Seinfeld
Secrets

An Insider Scoop About the Show

Author

Dennis Bjorklund

PRAETORIAN PUBLISHING

This publication is intended to provide accurate and authoritative information about the subject matter covered. It is sold with the understanding that the publisher does not render legal, accounting or other professional services. If legal advice or other expert assistance is required, seek the legal services of a competent professional.

Persons using this publication when dealing with specific legal matters should exercise discretion and their own independent judgment, and research original sources of authority and local court rules and procedures.

The publisher and author make no representations concerning the contents of this publication and disclaim any warranties of merchantability or fitness for a particular purpose, or any other liability for reliance upon the contents container herein.

This publication is merely the commencement of dialogue with the readers, and we welcome suggestions to update the book for reprint and future editions. Send all comments to the address hereinbelow.

Library of Congress Cataloging-in-Publication Data
Bjorklund, Dennis
    Seinfeld Secrets: An Insider Scoop About the Show

    1.   Seinfeld (Television program)   I.   Title.

    First published in the United States of America in 1998

TABLE OF CONTENTS

AUTHOR BIOGRAPHY

Author Dennis Bjorklund is an accomplished and well-respected television programming authority who published many small screen books covering some of the best sitcoms in network history. In addition to writing books, the Author provides literary contributions to numerous entertainment magazines and appears on E! Entertainment and Biography Channel as an authoritative expert.

Bjorklund is considered one of the foremost authorities on the television show Seinfeld and Cheers, and the only person to write thoroughly comprehensive books on these situation comedies. He continues to reside in California to remain close to the heart of network television programming.

The Author has written several books on these television shows. Here is the list of available books related to Cheers and Seinfeld:

Seinfeld Reference: The Complete Encyclopedia

Seinfeld Secrets: An Insider Scoop About the Show

Seinfeld Ultimate Episode Guide

Seinfeld Trivia: Everything About Nothing

Toasting Cheers: An Episode Guide to the 1982-1993 Series

Cheers TV Show: A Comprehensive Reference

Cheers Trivia: It's A Little Known Fact. . .

Check online or visit a local bookstore to purchase these and other titles written by Author Dennis Bjorklund.

THE ACTORS

Norman Brenner worked as Michael Richards' stand-in on the show for all nine seasons. Norman Brenner's entire acting resume is appearing in two titles: "Seinfeld" and "Curb Your Enthusiasm" (the "Seinfeld" episode). In "Seinfeld" he appeared in 28 episodes but only 5 were credited.

Deck McKenzie, who worked as Jerry Seinfeld's stand-in, portrayed George's colleague Bill in "The Revenge" (ep 12).

Barney Martin (Morty Seinfeld) worked as a policeman for 20 years before going into acting and appeared in a 1970s television commercial for Post Raisin Bran.

Len Lesser will be forever remembered as Uncle Leo in "Seinfeld" (1991-98). When he auditioned, Lesser received a lot of laughs from David, Seinfeld and casting director Marc Hirschfeld, but Lesser did not understand why because he did not think his lines were funny. Hirschfeld stated that when Lesser auditioned it was very clear that he was the right actor for the part.

Ruth Cohen (Monk's Diner cashier Ruthie Cohen) appears in 101 "Seinfeld" episodes (99 are uncredited), which is more than any other actor other than the four cast regulars. Her two credited roles are "The Gum" (ep 120) and "The Foundation" (ep 135).

Liz Sheridan (Helen Seinfeld) started in show business as a dancer, was engaged to James Dean in 1952, and wrote a book about their love, *Dizzy and Jimmy*.

Philip Sterling was originally cast as Jerry's father, Morty, but was replaced with Philip Bruns. Bruns was later replaced in the second season by Barney Martin because it was decided the character should be crankier. When the show went into syndication, Larry David wanted to reshoot Bruns's scenes with Martin but decided against the idea because the differences in the cast's ages would be noticeable.

Contrary to popular practice in sitcoms, Casting Director Marc Hirschfeld would often cast dramatic actors, like Peter Crombie (Joe Davola), for comedic roles. According to Hirschfled, "They understand it's important to commit to the character. Crombie was funny because he was so committed to being crazy."

THE SERIES

The original title to the show was "StandUp." It was supposed to be a 90-minute documentary to fill in for "Saturday Night Live" about how a comedian gets his material. Jerry never actually wanted a sitcom. When the idea developed into a sitcom, the title was "The Jerry Seinfeld Show." The title then evolved to "The Seinfeld Chronicles." However, when the show was renewed, the name was changed to "Seinfeld" to avoid confusion with another television program "The Marshall Chronicles" that debuted in the fall of 1990.

After the "Seinfeld" Pilot aired, NBC was not interested in renewing the show so it offered the series to Fox, which declined. Fortunately, Rick Ludwin, head of late night and special events for NBC, diverted money from his budget to film four episodes. This was the smallest sitcom order in television history.

The pilot features different title music, written by Jep Epstein, which was never used again. Thereafter Jonathon Wolff provided the trademark slap bass music. The theme song in the original version is different--it is a typical 80s-esque sitcom opening.

In the original pilot episode, some of the people in the studio audience were paid actors or extras. However, all the laughter is genuine.

The character Kramer did not appear in the first draft of the script. In early drafts, Kramer was named "Breckman," then "Hoffman," and later "Kessler" because of worries about the naming rights to "Kramer." At first the real-life inspiration for Kramer (Kenny Kramer) objected to using his name in the show. After the pilot, Jerry told Larry David that the name had to be Kramer because it sounded funnier (and less Jewish). After further negotiations a deal was stuck to name the character Kramer.

Tony Shalhoub ("Monk") auditioned for the part of Kramer.

Originally, the pilot featured George and Jerry as comedians with early versions of the script had George discussing his stand-up performance. However, this idea was abandoned, and George became a real estate broker. The character "George" was originally named "Bennett" after one of Larry David's college friends.

Julia Louis-Dreyfus' pregnancy during the 1991-92 season (Season 3) was concealed through camera angles, bulky clothing, or hiding behind objects. For example, throughout "The Subway" episode, Elaine is seen carrying a large wedding present in front of her stomach. When Julia went on maternity leave at the beginning of Season 4, Elaine's two-episode absence was explained through the other characters mentioning that she was vacationing in Europe.

Many characters were based upon real-life acquaintances, most notably John Peterman and George Steinbrenner. They also based characters on real-life individuals, such as the Soup Nazi (restauranteur Al Yeganeh) and Jackie Chiles (based upon attorney Johnnie L. Cochran, Jr.).

Some stories were inspired by headlines and rumors. For example, Kramer's lawsuit is roughly similar to the McDonald's coffee case ("The Maestro"). Jerry being "outed" as gay was based mainly on rumors about Jerry Seinfeld's sexuality ("The Outing"). Kramer having seizures at the sound of Mary Hart's voice was based upon a medically document case study ("The Good Samaritan").

Product placement for Snapple was inserted to mock the increasingly common practice of TV shows featuring a product to increase programming revenue.

The series does not have an opening credits sequence. Instead, the lead actor credits play out over a scene. Now commonplace in sitcoms and drama series, this was considered a novelty in 1990 and sparked a debate over the future of opening credits in a TV series.

The only script never filmed was written by Larry Charles and entitled, "The Bet" (aka "The Gun"). It involved Jerry betting $100 that Elaine would not buy a handgun to protect herself. Elaine ends up buying a gun from a friend of Kramer's. The cast, especially Julia Louis-Dreyfus, objected to this idea and the episode was only partially filmed. In a subplot, Kramer returns from a vacation in Puerto Rico and tells Jerry and George that he had sex with a flight attendant during the flight back. George makes a bet with him and they go to the airport with Jerry and Elaine to ask the flight attendant if Kramer's allegation is true.

The episode was written by Larry Charles to make a funny "dark-theme" episode, using elements that were unusual in sitcoms. Sets for the episode were built, while Bobbi Jo Lathan was cast as flight attendant (Lucy Merrit) and Ernie Sabella as the gun salesman (Mo Korn), described in the script as "overweight, greasy, slow and low-key." The table reading of the episode was held on Wednesday, December 12, 1990.

In one of the scenes Elaine holds a gun and says, "Where do you want it, Jerry? [holds the gun to her head] The Kennedy? [holds the gun to her stomach] The McKinley?" (referencing the assassination of the two American presidents). After reading her scene, Julia Louis-Dreyfus said, "I'm not doing this." Both Alexander and episode director Tom Cherones felt the gun content in the story was too provocative. Michael Richards was concerned that his character would be open about arming Elaine, though in a later interview he stated "although, why not? I think Kramer could justify the use of a weapon."

The cast began rehearsing, but after 20 minutes stopped and turned to Cherones, who agreed to talk to Charles. They met with NBC executives and the creators and decided to scrap the episode. The replacement episode, "The Phone Message," was written by David and Seinfeld in two days. Both Lathan and Sabella were given roles in later episodes: Lathan appeared as Patti in "The Stranded" (ep 27) while Sabella was cast as the "greasy naked guy" in "The Subway" (ep 30).

According to Spike Feresten, when pitching episode ideas to Larry and Jerry, the creators want to hear stories, not pitches. He was discussing "The Soup Nazi" merely as part of the conversation or as an anecdote and they said, "Write that first." Feresten was not expecting it to be an episode plot. According to Peter Mehlman, each writer came up with their own story lines or they were gone. There was no writers' room. It was the only show to use this writing process.

In Season Two, "Seinfeld" aired opposite the second half of "Jake and the Fatman," which routinely beat the struggling NBC sitcom. According to Jerry, viewers turned the channel to see the second half because that was the part of the show where the Fatman had to run.

Although "Seinfeld" struggled in the Nielsen ratings the first couple years, everything changed when it moved to Thursday night after "Cheers" in 1993. TV Ratings: 1992-93: #25; 1993-94: #3; 1994-95: #1; 1995-96: #2; 1996-97: #2; 1997-98: #1.

Castle Rock took a poll of the top 10 episodes; they were (in no specific order): The Contest, The Soup Nazi, The Junior Mint, The Opposite, The Hamptons, The Parking Garage, The Chicken Roaster, The Bubble Boy, The Outing, and The Marine Biologist.

Pilot

"The Seinfeld Chronicles"

Season Regulars

Jerry Seinfeld (Jerry Seinfeld), Michael Richards (Kessler), Lee Garlington (Claire), Jason Alexander (George Costanza)

1. "Good News, Bad News" (7.5.89)

For syndication, the pilot episode was re-titled "Good News, Bad News" to avoid confusion with season four's episode "The Pilot" (ep 63-64). Other titles considered for this episode were "Signals" and "The Airport Pick-Up." The production staff and writers refer to the pilot as "The Seinfeld Chronicles."

The featured diner is Pete's Luncheonette, which was changed to Monk's Diner for the remainder of the series. Pete's Luncheonette uses a set that had its exterior left over from *The Muppets Take Manhattan* (1984).

Kramer has a dog named Ralph that was included in the episode so Jerry Seinfeld could perform a stand-up routine about dogs. The routine was cut and the dog was never explained and did not appear in any future episodes.

Although listed as a cast regular, Lee Garlington (Claire) only appears in the first scene. Her role was a waitress who offered friendly advice to Jerry and George. In early scripts, Claire was originally called "Meg." After the pilot, NBC demanded a stronger female supporting role that would add more sex appeal to the show. Consequently, the character Elaine Benes was introduced in the second filmed episode, "Male Unbonding" (ep 4).

A deleted scene from the pilot episode features Jerry and George driving to the airport, where they talk about changing lanes on the road and giving "thank you waves." This concept was reused in later episodes "The Good Samaritan" (ep 37) and "The Puerto Rican Day" (ep 176). Some parts of the stand-up material featured in the pilot were filmed for "The Ex-Girlfriend" (ep 6) but eventually deleted from the episode.

Season 1: 1989-1990

Season Regulars
Jerry Seinfeld (Jerry Seinfeld), Julia Louis-Dreyfus (Elaine Benes), Michael Richards (Kramer), Jason Alexander (George Costanza)

2. "The Stakeout" (5.31.90)

In an early draft of the script, Morty Seinfeld was named "Leon" and Helen was referred to as "Mother." His name was changed to"Morty" at some point during the production week.

This episode contains the first mention of George's favorite alias Art Vandelay and his desire to be an architect.

This is Elaine's first appearance. Her name was originally Eileen. The name was changed a few days before filming the episode. Although this is the second episode to air, it was the third to be produced. It was decided that it should air second because it provided background information about Elaine and her relationship with Jerry.

The plot is drawn from an incident in Larry David's life. David went to a restaurant with a woman he previously dated (Monica Yates) and met another woman. He could not flirt as much as he wanted due to the presence of Yates. David only knew the name of the building where she worked and staked it out.

Brandon Tartikoff kept a scene from this episode cued up on his office VCR to show visitors the pure humor of "Seinfeld."

The fictional law firm "Sagman, Bennett, Robbins, Oppenheim and Taft" uses the names of Larry David's college friends. Vanessa, the woman Jerry desires, was the name of a woman David once dated.

Due to a limited budget, the "poor man's process" was used for the taxi scene where crew members shake the car and flash lights overhead to give the illusion of movement along a city street. It was actually filmed in a studio using a black background.

In the video store scene, extras are seen stepping down from the front of the stage.

3. "The Robbery" (6.7.90)

The idea for the episode was inspired by Seinfeld's real-life experience where his apartment was robbed when he was a student. Instead of the door being unlocked (as it was in the episode), the burglars broke through the wall. Seinfeld has since commented that it was like being robbed by Superman.

Kramer makes his first sliding entrance in this episode. According to Michael Richards, he was late on his cue so he compensated by coming in very fast. When the audience laughed, Richards decided to keep the sliding entrance and it eventually became a trademark.

While warming up the audience, Seinfeld improvised the routine about someone giving the middle finger as an offensive act. It worked so well that it was used in the opening stand-up segment instead of his prepared material.

Carolyn the waitress and her husband Larry are named after Seinfeld's real-life sister and brother-in-law.

In an early draft of the script, Jerry's English neighbor is named "Berbick," the man Kramer accuses of stealing Jerry's property.

4. "Male Unbonding" (6.14.90)

"Male Unbonding" was the second episode produced. In early drafts of the script, Elaine does not appear. The character was added during pre-production and therefore Elaine appears in only one scene.

Other than the pilot, this is the only episode not starting with the word "The" in the title. Although it was common practice to have humorous titles, Larry David wanted the writers to focus on the episode material because the title would not be known to many viewers. This practice caught-on with other shows, such as "Friends" that started every episode title with "The One...."

Jerry's audience monologues were recorded twice. The first time he appeared in front of a piano in a brightly lit room that resembled a church basement. The monologue was re-recorded in front of a dark curtain to give the feel of a night club performance.

An alternate ending was filmed where Joel asks Jerry if he can date Elaine. Jerry is offended and breaks up with Joel for good. Joel storms out of the diner but returns to say that he will see Jerry the following week to return the k.d. lang tape he borrowed. Jerry then refers to Joel as Jason from the *Friday the 13th* movie franchise.

Kevin Dunn (Jerry's childhood friend, Joel) auditioned for the role of George Costanza.

5. "The Stock Tip" (6.21.90)

This was the last "Seinfeld" episode to be filmed at Ren-Mar Studios in Hollywood. All future episodes were filmed at CBS Studio Center in Studio City, California.

Soon after this episode aired, NBC executives ordered 12 additional "Seinfeld" episodes to air as a mid-season replacement during the 1990-91 season.

During filming, Michael Richards played a practical joke on the rest of the cast. He entered Jerry's apartment with a woman who immediately began removing her clothes until she had stripped down to a g-string.

An earlier draft of the episode featured Jerry arguing that during a nuclear holocaust, when everyone is very depressed, Superman could cheer everyone up with his "super humor." George responded by saying that no-one would laugh because they would blame Superman for not stopping the holocaust in the first place.

A line cut from the finished episode had Jerry agreeing to let Kramer's anarchist friends stay in his place but only if they promised to wear all of Jerry's underwear.

Season 2: 1990-1991

Season Regulars
Jerry Seinfeld (Jerry Seinfeld), Julia Louis-Dreyfus (Elaine Benes), Michael Richards (Kramer), Jason Alexander (George Costanza)

6. "The Ex-Girlfriend" (1.23.91)

As with most of the early episodes, it was inspired when Larry David gave a ride home to a woman who had recently dated his friend. He was conflicted about breaking up with her because the sex was too good.

Among the actresses who auditioned for the part of Marlene: Amy Yasbeck ("Wings"), Jeri Ryan ("Star Trek: Voyager") and Heidi Swedberg (who later played Susan Ross in "Seinfeld").

Norman Brenner, Michael Richards' stand-in, appears as an extra during the second scene, walking by twice in different clothing.

Due to a limited budget, the "poor man's process" was used for the car scenes where crew members shake the car and flash lights overhead to give the illusion of movement along a city street.

This episode was supposed to air on January 16, 1991 but its premiere was postponed one week due to the start of the first Gulf War.

Beginning with this episode, "Seinfeld" was filmed before a live studio audience on stage 19 of the CBS/MTM lot in Studio City, California.

Some scenes in the episode were cut or changed prior to broadcast. The opening scene in Jerry's car, in which George discusses breaking up with Marlene, originally had George proposing that he would stage his own kidnapping while walking down the street with Marlene, and then hide out until she had given up on him. Another scene which was cut featured Kramer entering Jerry's apartment carrying a plate with cantaloupe on toothpicks. In addition, the original scene where Jerry tells George that he is dating Marlene took place in a library, with a librarian repeatedly shushing the pair, and kicking them out of the library at the end of the scene. The location was changed to Monk's Diner because the dialogue had nothing to do with a library.

7. "The Pony Remark" (1.30.91)

This episode was based on a remark Larry David made during a conversation that caused a commotion with another guest.

In the first draft of the episode, Morty and Helen Seinfeld were only referred to as "Father" and Mother." In a later draft, Morty was called "Leon."

In an early draft for this episode, Jerry's mother was named Adele. However, this did not match her name from "The Stake Out" (ep 2) so it was later changed back to Helen.

Jerry is left-handed, yet his baseball glove is for a right-handed player. The prop department did not have a glove for left-handed players.

Tom Cherones deliberately made Elaine sit at a smaller table while directing the dinner scene.

At the funeral, Elaine callously asks Isaac about the status of his old apartment. This idea was added during rehearsals.

8. "The Jacket" (2.6.91)

The storyline is based upon Larry David's personal experience when he was dating Monica Yates, who wanted him to meet her father, Richard Yates, a respected novelist. David had just bought a suede jacket, and met Richard Yates at the Algonquin Hotel. Mr. Yates was austere and intimidating like Alton Benes. David ultimately ruined a suede jacket when they headed out to the restaurant in the snow.

Lawrence Tierney (Elaine's father, Alton Benes) had a notorious reputation for drunkenness, barroom brawls and intimidating coworkers. He was originally cast as a recurring character but his volatility terrified the cast and crew; they did not want him back. According to the producers, Tierney took a knife from the set and hid it under his jacket. When Jerry Seinfeld confronted him, Tierney pulled the knife to imitate the famous shower scene and score from *Psycho* claiming he was going to use it during a scene as a joke. Afterwards, Larry David would jokingly threaten to have Tierney back on the show if the crew was getting out of line.

This is the only episode to mention Elaine's mother. Louis-Dreyfus once suggested Mary Tyler Moore to portray Elaine's mother, but the character never appeared on the show.

The episode also contains the first mention of Elaine's job as a manuscript reader for Pendant Publishing. In early drafts of the script she worked as an optician.

This episode originally had a reference to serial killer Gary Gilmore's last words, "Let's do it." The scene was changed during the final shoot. In the deleted scene, Jerry is trying to decide whether to buy the jacket when he finally remarks to Elaine, "Well, in the immortal words of Gary Gilmore 'Let's do it.'"

In this episode, Kramer's misadventure with the doves, which we hear about but never see, is later mentioned in "The Stranded" (ep 27). In early drafts, the final scene had Kramer entering Jerry's house with a dove on his shoulder.

Ryan Stiles ("The Drew Carey Show") auditioned to play the clothing store attendant.

9. "The Phone Message" (2.13.91)

The plot is based on a real-life experience of Larry David. He once tried replacing an answering machine tape with a blank cassette to remove an embarrassing message that would mean the end of his relationship. David previously wrote a skit for "Saturday Night Live" about a man entering his girlfriend's house to erase her answering machine. It was never produced, which allowed David to use the storyline for "Seinfeld."

Jerry's storyline was based on Seinfeld's personal disdain for the cotton Dockers commercials.

This episode was written in two days. It was a hurried project to replace the controversial episode, "The Bet" (aka "The Gun").

A few changes were made to the first few drafts of the script. Additional dialogue between George and Jerry regarding dates during the 1850s was removed for timing purposes. During his date with Donna, Jerry would mention his remark about ponies in the earlier episode "The Pony Remark" (ep 7) but this was later changed to remark about leaving a note when committing suicide. Initially, Kramer's first name was revealed in the episode; though the information was removed from the eventual script. The idea of revealing Kramer's first name would be further exploited in"The Switch" (ep 97).

Gina Hecht auditioned for the part of Donna (Jerry's girlfriend who liked Dockers commercials). She later portrays George's psychiatrist Dana Foley in "The Pilot" (ep 63).

Despite critical acclaim, only 13 million viewers saw the episode, making it #59 in the Nielsen ratings. The ratings were so low that "Seinfeld" was put on hiatus for two months and considered for cancellation because the typical audience size should be 18-22 million viewers. Fortunately, the series was positioned after "Cheers" where it earned significantly higher ratings and increased popularity leading NBC to order a full season of episodes.

10.   "The Apartment" (4.4.91)

After reading a few articles Peter Mehlman had written for *The New York Times* and *Esquire*, the "Seinfeld" creators asked him to write an episode. Mehlman had no dialogue writing experience but conceived the idea where Elaine moved away and Jerry had to confront his feelings about her. The creators and staff writer Larry Charles thought it would be funnier if Elaine would move closer to Jerry instead. As Mehlman was writing the script, he came up with the idea of George wearing a wedding ring to a party to gauge how women react. Though the wedding ring idea was not included in the approved script, Seinfeld and David decided to keep it in the episode because it suited George.

This is the first episode where Elaine does her "Get out!" shove. The catchphrase was not in the original script but added at Louis-Dreyfus' suggestion.

Louis-Dreyfus' half-sister Lauren Bowles appears as an extra at the brunch party. Bowles would continue to appear regularly throughout the series' run, frequently as a waitress at Monk's Diner.

Joan Van Horn's only acting role was this episode (feeding her baby in Monk's Diner). She worked on "Seinfeld" as a unit production manager, first assistant director, and line producer.

The scene where Jerry informs George that he told Elaine about the apartment was initially shot with them standing in line at the movies and talking about sitting in the front of the theater. George would tell Jerry that he once pretended to have a grotesque physical impairment while he was standing in line to get a ticket for *The Exorcist* (1973), and people would let him go in front of them without saying anything. The location of this scene, however, was changed to Monk's Diner, and their dialogue was shortened. In the original script, Jerry, instead of George, proclaimed himself "lord of the idiots," but this was changed during rehearsals.

This episode was the show's return to air after a two-month hiatus during which it was considered for cancellation. But it's new time slot after "Cheers" helped boost the show's Nielsen ratings and get it renewed for a third season. It was watched in 15.7 million homes, making it the ninth most-watched program of the week it was broadcast. The episode gained mostly positive responses from critics. The "Cheers" audience was 20.5 million homes. "Seinfeld's" ability to keep a large number of the "Cheers" audience eventually helped the show get a thirteen episode order for the fall of 1991.

11. "The Statue" (4.11.91)

The episode contained numerous references to the 1960s television crime drama "Dragnet" because episodic writer Larry Charles watched numerous reruns of the show when writing for "Seinfeld." Kramer pretends to be Joe Friday, the central character of "Dragnet." Charles was interesting in further developing the Kramer character and used this episode to showcase Michael Richards' talents. Richards cites this episode and "The Revenge" (ep 12) as episodes that really defined the Kramer character.

"Seinfeld" writer's assistant Karen Wilkie can be seen in the audience during Jerry Seinfeld's stand-up comedy act. She also appeared in four uncredited "Seinfeld" episodes.

Nurit Koppel portrayed Rava, however, Jane Leeves ("Frasier" 1993–2004), who would later appear as Marla the Virgin, auditioned for the part.

Michael D. Conway played the part of Ray Thomas; however, Hank Azaria and Tony Shalhoub also auditioned for the part.

Norman Brenner, who worked as Michael Richards' stand-in, appears as an extra in the background when Jerry and Ray talk at Monk's Diner.

George breaks the original statue singing the song "MacArthur Park" by Donna Summer, but the original script had him singing Eddie Cochran's "There Ain't No Cure for the Summertime Blues."

In an early draft, Elaine sits by George to eavesdrop on Jerry and Ray's conversation. She wears a floppy hat to look inconspicuous and complains that she looks like one of the Cowsills (a singing group in 1960s and 1970s). The same scene initially featured George admitting that he spied on Ray a day earlier, showing Ray pictures of him in a bar. Ray replies it was his day off and asks why George was not at work; George replies that he should be getting back and leaves. In the original script, Elaine and Rava argue over who is a better person: Jerry or Ray.

12. "The Revenge" (4.18.91)

The episode's main plot-line (George quitting his job and going back the next day pretending nothing happened) is based on Larry David's personal experience when he was a writer on "Saturday Night Live." He angrily quit halfway through the 1984-1985 television season when they cut his sketches, but regretted the decision once he was home. His neighbor, Kenny Kramer, suggested returning to work the following day and act as if nothing had happened. Unlike George Costanza, the ploy succeeded for David, who remained with SNL's writing staff until the end of that season.

George being barred from the bathroom was inspired by "Seinfeld" writer Larry Charles who often used the private restroom in Seinfeld and David's office, instead of the public one, which upset the creators. The subplot of Newman feigned suicide was inspired by one of David's neighbors who once jumped from the second floor of their apartment building. Newman was originally meant to appear on camera in this episode but the role eventually became an off-camera character voiced by Larry David. Wayne Knight re-recorded all of Newman's lines for syndication.

This is the first episode where Michael Richards begins using physical comedy as part of his character's persona. He insisted on using real cement in the washing machine in order to portray the actual physical comedy of managing a heavy object. During the first take Richards fell through a door and it had to be filmed again.

A number of scenes in the episode were removed prior to broadcast, such as one in which George and Kramer meet in the hallway and Kramer informs George that Jerry has gone to the laundromat. The writers decided that George could just say Kramer told him Jerry was at the laundromat and, upon that addition, the scene was cut. Initially, during Jerry and George's conversation about jobs, George mentions Regis Philbin, when they discuss George being a talk show host. Additional dialogue between George and Jerry at the laundromat was also removed. Because the episode "The Stranded" (ep 27) did not air until mid season three, a few references to that episode also had to be cut.

The Newman subplot was significantly reduced; the character initially appeared in one scene, but it was never filmed. Auditions were held for the role. It came down to Tim Russ ("Star Trek: Voyager") and William Thomas, Jr. ("The Cosby Show"). Thomas was cast for the part. In the scene, Newman explained to Jerry and Kramer that he jumped from the roof but an awning broke his fall, though Jerry and Kramer remain skeptical. The episode also involved the second appearance of Harold the building superintendent, "The Apartment" (ep 10), informing the main characters that Newman made up the story about the awning breaking his fall. However, with the reduction of Newman's subplot, the scene was removed.

Deck McKenzie, who plays George's coworker Bill, worked as Jerry Seinfeld's stand-in and appeared in 13 "Seinfeld" episodes (6 uncredited).

Mr. Papanickolas, who is mentioned by Kramer but unseen, was named after Pete Papanickolas, who worked as the key grip on the "Seinfeld" production crew.

13.   "The Heart Attack" (4.25.91)

"Seinfeld" writer Larry Charles had his tonsils removed when he was younger but they grew back. This became the basis for the story line.

Stephen Tobolowsky (Tor Eckman) faced death many times in his life: he broke his neck in five places horseback riding, was held hostage, had a gun pulled on him, and was stabbed. He also turned down the role of Al on "Home Improvement."

Larry David has an uncredited role as the B-movie actor whose vexing lines ("Flaming globes of Zigmund") infiltrate Jerry's subconscious causing him to scribble a potential comedy bit.

Pat Hazell, who plays the man in the other hospital bed, was a special consultant to the show and regularly did the audience warm-up during the first couple seasons. He also appeared in "The Pilot, Part 2" (ep 64).

14.   "The Deal" (5.2.91)

The plot was based on a real life experience of Larry David where he and woman tried to make rules to govern a physical relationship without the emotional attachment and still keeping their friendship.

This was originally written as the last episode of the series. Larry David expected the series to be canceled so he wrote an episode having Jerry and Elaine reuniting, which is what NBC executive Warren Littlefield was urging David to do all year. The ploy worked to help convince NBC to renew "Seinfeld" for another year. Naturally, as a jab at NBC, Larry David promptly ended the romance and it was never mentioned again.

Ironically, NBC showed the final four episodes of the second season out of order. This episode was fourth from the last, so the final three episodes, having been made before this one, made no reference to Jerry and Elaine dating. And after the show was picked up for a third year, no further reference was made to Jerry and Elaine and their one episode reunion.

During his stand-up performances, Seinfeld asked the audience if the Jerry-Elaine relationship should continue, and the answer was always a resounding "No." Larry David agreed and it was decided that Jerry and Elaine would no longer be romantically involved.

15. "The Baby Shower" (5.16.91)

The episode was partly based on a friend of Larry Charles who was pregnant but did not want to experience childbirth so she asked the doctor to anesthetize her, which Charles thought ironic.

This episode was the first to showcase the primary storylines of all four characters coming together in the final scene. The other was "The Busboy" (ep 17) (which was technically the first because it was filmed prior to "The Baby Shower").

In early drafts of the script, the episode opened with Kramer telling Jerry about the Russian cable installers while Elaine and Jerry would realize ahead of time that the baby shower and the cable installation would take place at the same time. This was changed as the writers felt it would be better left as a surprise. Some dialogue was removed from the scene, as Kramer initially told Jerry that Benjamin Franklin would have wanted free cable. Additional dialogue between the baby shower guests regarding turning off men was also cut.

The baby shower scene where Mary Cantardi berates Jerry for never calling her after their date was not in the original script. It was added during rehearsals to give Jerry more involvement in the final scene.

The episode also contains a dream sequence where Jerry is killed; Charles was interested in "the Quentin Tarantino version of a sitcom."

The character Leslie was largely based on Karen Finley and Johanna Went, two performance artists who use food in their act.

16.   "The Chinese Restaurant" (5.23.91)

Larry David came up with the idea of the real-time episode while he and Jerry Seinfeld were waiting for a table at a Chinese restaurant in Los Angeles.

This episode was originally scheduled to air months earlier but was held back by the network. NBC was uncomfortable with a real-time episode, only having one set, and lacking a storyline. Executive Warren Littlefield commented that he thought there were pages missing from the script he received. David argued that each character had a storyline--Jerry' recognizes a woman but cannot recall how he knows her; Elaine is ravenously hungry; George' needs to use the phone to resolve an issue with his girlfriend. NBC disagreed. To satisfy the executives, writer Larry Charles suggested the group's storyline include the urgency of getting to a one-night screening of *Plan 9 from Outer Space*, thereby introducing a "ticking clock" scenario to the story. When the NBC executives still objected, David threatened to quit the show if the network would force any major changes upon the script. NBC allowed the episode to be produced but postponed the air date beyond the season finale date of other TV shows. Naturally, as a jab to NBC, the network's response was subsequently parodied in "The Pitch" (ep 43).

The original script had Jerry, George, and Elaine and Jerry picking their least favorite holiday as they enter the restaurant. Jerry picked New Year's Eve, George picked Halloween, and Elaine picked the Fourth of July. In the version that aired, they talk about combining the jobs of policemen and garbage men into a single job. In the original draft, the three friends also discussed how to spend any future long-waiting periods: George suggests bringing a deck of cards while Jerry recommended bringing a jigsaw puzzle with nothing but penguins. One scene was cut before broadcast--George explaining to Jerry that he pulled his hamstring while trying to untuck the covers of a hotel bed during his recent stay in Boston. George can be seen grabbing his hamstring as he walks to the phone.

Kramer does not appear in this episode. At this point in the series, it was established that Kramer had not left the apartment building in many years. Michael Richards expressed his disappointment at not being included in the episode because he felt it was the series' best episode at the time.

In the restaurant when Elaine walks up to the table to grab an egg-roll and explains the bet, the people at the table begin to talk among themselves. Larry David makes an uncredited appearance as a customer at the table pestered by Elaine, saying "Someone tell me what she said! What did she say?"

In the Nielsen ratings, Seinfeld was the eighteenth most-watched show of the week, and the sixth most-watched show on NBC. NBC executives held a meeting after the broadcast to determine the fate of the show, and decided it would receive a third season order if the writers would put more effort into episode storylines.

17.   "The Busboy" (6.26.91)

This is the only episode that does not include a story for Jerry. After it was recorded, Castle Rock executive Glenn Padnick approached the star to inform him that he was being too generous to his co-stars and told to always include material for his own character.

This episode was a major turning point for the series. It was the literal intersection of the two major storylines at the end of the episode (the fight between Elaine's boyfriend and the restaurant busboy). Larry David never thought to do this previously and became enamored with the idea. It would become a "Seinfeld" trademark. This was the third episode produced in Season 2, but the last episode to air.

Though considered a classic "Elaine" episode, actress Julia Louis-Dreyfus disliked her acting in the episode, noting that the "deadpan stare" in the Rockaway Boulevard shortcut scene was a bad choice.

This episode was filmed in November 1990 but did not air until June 1991, making George's winter clothes a bit anachronistic on its broadcast premiere.

The exterior stock footage used for the busboy's building at 1324 Amsterdam Avenue was also used as the home of holistic healer Tor Eckman in "The Heart Attack" (ep 13).

Season 3: 1991-1992

Season Regulars
Jerry Seinfeld (Jerry Seinfeld), Julia Louis-Dreyfus (Elaine Benes), Michael Richards (Kramer), Jason Alexander (George Costanza)

18. "The Note" (9.18.91)

Other than the original pilot, this is the only episode with a different version of the theme song, using female back-up singers harmonizing over the iconic slap-bass tune. Composer Jonathan Wolff added the singers because Jerry Seinfeld wanted to add "a little sparkle" to the music and suggested the addition of some scat lyrics. The creators liked the additions, and three episodes were produced with the new style music. However, they never informed NBC or Castle Rock of the change, and when the season premiere aired, the executives were surprised and unimpressed, and demanded a switch to the original style. The next two episodes were changed prior to airing, leaving this episode as the only one with the additional music elements.

Joshua Liebling, who plays Billy the physical therapist's son, is Jerry Seinfeld's real-life nephew.

In early scripts the dentist character was named Lloyd but later changed to Roy (but not in the credits).

This episode was the first with the new Seinfeld logo.

19. "The Truth" (9.25.91)

This is the first "Seinfeld" episode written by a woman. Elaine Pope wrote with Larry David and Larry Charles on "Fridays," a short-lived ABC sketch show (comparable to "Saturday Night Live") with a cast including Larry David and Michael Richards.

20. "The Pen" (10.2.91)

The plot was partly inspired by a sofa bed in the Delray Beach retirement community condo owned by Jerry's mother, Betty. During stays, Jerry would place couch cushions on the floor and sleep on them to avoid the uncomfortable sofa bed mattress.

Larry David learned about the pen that writes upside down from executive producer George Shapiro who owned one. Shapiro was showing it off during a meeting and then gave the pen to David.

This is the only episode not to feature either George or Kramer in any of its scenes. Jason Alexander was furious with Larry David for not writing him into this episode, and insisted that he must be in every future show, even just for a bit part.

21. "The Dog" (10.9.91)

The character Gavin Polone (the drunken man on the plane) is named after Larry David's manager. Farfel the dog is named after a puppet that appeared in ads for Nestle's Quik in the 1950s and 60s. In one scene, Elaine is making chocolate milk.

Elaine wants Jerry to accompany her to see the film, *Prognosis: Negative*, which is the name of Larry David's unproduced screenplay where the main character wrongly assumes a negative medical prognosis is a bad thing. Nevertheless, David still worked the idea into a script. In "The Pilot, Part 2" (ep 64), George misinterprets a conversation with his doctor; after being told the medical test results were negative, George freaks out until the doctor assures him that negative is good news.

22. "The Library" (10.16.91)

The character Sandy is referred as Sherry in this episode. The name was changed in the final script but that was after the credits were set.

Harris Shore played the role of Mr. Lippman in this episode. Richard Fancy took over the role for the remainder of the series.

23.   "The Parking Garage" (10.30.91)

In the original script, the episode was supposed to end with the cast driving out of the parking garage. However, when they shot the scene, the car would not start. When viewing the episode, Elaine and Kramer are laughing uncontrollably. The creators decided to leave the unexpected ending because it offered a more humorous result and another example of everything going wrong that day.

This episode was difficult to write and create because it all had to be done on the normal "Seinfeld" soundstage. Jerry's apartment and the studio audience seating had to be removed. Every shot used showed the entire set so it constantly required shooting from different angles. Mirrors all around the perimeters of the stage gave the illusion of further depth and with just a dozen cars the illusion of being in a giant parking garage was complete. The live studio audience for "The Tape" (ep 25) was also shown "The Parking Garage;" their laughter was recorded and then used as the laugh track for this episode.

You can see Michael Richards really hit his head on the air conditioning box as he puts it into the car trunk. In the last few shots of the episode he has a noticeable fat lip. The accident may have been less severe had he not insisted that the prop department put a real air conditioner in the box. Richards wanted to make his struggle with the box seem genuine. He made the same request when using a bag of cement in "The Revenge" (ep 12).

The exterior shots of the parking garage are of the Newport Centre Mall in Jersey City, New Jersey.

Kramer casually mentions that he is wearing a jacket that was left at his mother's house by a guy she was dating. This jacket would become a plot point in the next three episodes.

"Seinfeld" writer Larry Charles has a cameo in this episode as the man with the long beard who ignores Elaine when she asks for help.

24. "The Cafe" (11.6.91)

Babu Bhatt was originally named as "Vong Sim" in early drafts of the script, though actors of all ethnicities auditioned for the role.

Six actors auditioned for the role of the "Angry Man's Voice," but the part ended up going to Deck Mackenzie who also worked as Jerry's stand-in.

This is the first episode to have applause by the studio audience as Kramer entered. It happened when Kramer entered the Dream Cafe rather than Jerry's apartment.

25. "The Tape" (11.13.91)

The Chinese baldness cure is based on something Larry David tried in real life. The video footage Kramer takes of George's scalp are identical to those the real Kenny Kramer took of Larry David.

Jerry refers to Abbott and Costello in this episode. "The Abbott and Costello Show" is often cited as an inspiration for the tone of "Seinfeld."

Beder, a character who calls Jerry over during the show's first coffee shop scene, is played by Norman Brenner. Brenner worked behind the scenes as Kramer's stand-in. Internet fans of Seinfeld enjoy playing "Where's Norman?" as they attempt to identify his every appearance as an extra during the show's nine seasons.

26. "The Nose Job" (11.20.91)

This episode was derived from Jerry's personal experience when his sister Carolyn considered getting a nose job. She was self-conscious about her appearance and has been described as homely. A friend convinced Carolyn to undergo the procedure and it vastly improved her appearance.

Tawny Kitaen appeared in this episode because of her ongoing romance with Jerry Seinfeld. The romance faded quickly when she was impregnated by an ex-boyfriend. Kitaen is best remembered as the sexy vixen in several Whitesnake videos when dating/married to the lead singer David Coverdale.

Susan Diol (large-nosed Audrey) was married to successful television director Andy Cadiff ("Hot in Cleveland," "My Wife and Kids," "Spin City" and "Home Improvement") and 70s teen idol Shaun Cassidy (TV "Hardy Boys" and #1 song "Da Doo Ron Ron").

27.   "The Stranded" (11.27.91)

Although aired in season three, this episode was originally intended to air in season two. The broadcast included a special introduction by Jerry to explain the continuity error caused by airing the episode out of sequence. The episode was postponed because Larry David was dissatisfied with the script and shelved it for nearly a year. It was advertised as a "lost" episode.

Michael Chiklis (Long Island party host Steve) is well-recognized in *Fantastic Four* movies, "The Shield" and "The Commish" (1991-96).

Elaine (Julia Louis-Dreyfus) fakes a porn star audition while Jerry (Jerry Seinfeld) assists and Kramer (Michael Richards) films in "The Tape."

28. "The Alternate Side" (12.4.91)

The idea for a Woody Allen storyline came from Larry David's personal experiences. David briefly appeared in Allen's movies *Radio Days* (1987) and *New York Stories* (1989), and would later have the lead role in *Whatever Works* (2009). Allen is one of Larry David's favorite comedians.

Jerry Seinfeld credits the phrase, "These pretzels are making me thirsty," as the first of the show's many catch-phrases. During his next stand-up tour, audience members would chant this during virtually every performance.

Larry David has an uncredited voice role as the car thief.

Though never referred to by name, the rental car agent is called "Lydia" in the script.

George wears a jersey with "Broadway Bound" on it in the first scene. Jason Alexander played Stanley in the original Broadway cast of Neil Simon's play *Broadway Bound*.

29. "The Red Dot" (12.11.91)

David Naughton (Elaine's alcoholic boyfriend, Dick) was the singer/dancer in the 1970s Dr. Pepper ads, had a hit disco single "Makin' It" (#5 in 1979), starred in the TV show of the same name (1979) and costarred in "My Sister Sam" (1986-88) as Jack Kincaid (opposite Pam Dawber and Rebecca Schaeffer).

Richard Fancy makes his debut appearance as Mr. Lippman, Elaine's boss at Pendant Publishing. He would continue in the role for the show's remaining six seasons.

Though it never appeared in any episode, Jerry has been doing yoga every morning for years.

30. "The Subway" (1.8.92)

In this episode, Jerry has an opening monologue of a father-son duo commandeering a bumper car. This bit mirrors a comedy routine he used in the unaired TV pilot "Celebrity Cabaret" (1977).

Julia Louis-Dreyfus was pregnant during season three, and her expanding mid-section was becoming more visible by the time this episode was filmed. The creators concealed the pregnancy by having her hide behind objects, such as a large wedding gift in this episode.

Every scene in the four different subway cars was actually shot in a single car on the "Seinfeld" soundstage. The logos and signs inside the car were redressed and removed around, and the extras were moved into different places to give the illusion that the single rented subway car was actually four separate cars going in four separate directions. To create the illusion of a rocking subway ride, several stagehands stood on either side of the car's outside walls and rocked it back and forth with 2x4s. The set was on loan to NBC from another studio, and on the set's return to its original soundstage, the truck carrying the set accidentally destroyed it while traveling under an overpass that was too low. The set was rebuilt and is still used.

Michael Wrona has an uncredited voice role as the track announcer. He currently serves as the track announcer at Golden Gate Fields.

"Seinfeld" writer Peter Mehlman has a cameo appearance as a subway rider during the scenes where we hear Elaine's thoughts.

The horse that Kramer bets on, Papanick, was named after the show's key grip, Pete Papanickolas.

31.   "The Pez Dispenser" (1.15.92)
Larry David wrote most of "The Pez Dispenser" while supervising the production of the previous episode, "The Subway."

32.   "The Suicide" (1.29.92)
Peggy Lane O'Rourke (Nurse) has a small role in 12 "Seinfeld" episodes (6 aired parts, 5 scenes deleted and unaired, 1 voice role, and 4 stand-in roles). She also had 7 small roles in "King of Queens." She was the lead stand-in for Elaine from 1991-98.

Jason Alexander's mother appears as an extra sitting on a bench next to Elaine.

Wayne Knight makes his first appearance as Newman. He once auditioned for the role of George Costanza.

In this episode, Jerry mentions that George's father is bald. In "The Handicap Spot" (ep 62) George's father (Frank) was played by John Randolph, who was bald. However, when Jerry Stiller, who is not bald, took over the role of Frank the following year, Randolph's scenes were reshot with Stiller. Therefore, the line about George's father being bald is a continuity error.

In his scene with the psychic, George mentions that his brother once impregnated a woman named Pauline. His brother is mentioned only one other time and then is forgotten by the time we meet George's mother in "The Contest" (ep 51).

33.   "The Fix-up" (2.5.92)

Maggie Jakobson (Cynthia) is also known as Maggie Wheeler. She is best known for the irritating voice and laugh of Janice in "Friends." She unsuccessfully auditioned for the role of Monica in "Friends," Debra in "Everybody Loves Raymond," and Vicki in "Suddenly Susan."

Julia Louis-Dreyfus's off-screen pregnancy meant that her character had to spend the latter half of this season hiding her belly behind furniture and laundry baskets.

34-35. "The Boyfriend, Part 1 & 2" (2.12.92)

Keith Hernandez was a star first baseman for the New York Mets from 1983-89, won 11 consecutive Gold Glove Awards, and National League MVP in 1979. If Hernandez had turned them down they would have asked Gary Carter to take his place. Darryl Strawberry was supposed to play the "Second Spitter" but due to his then-recent drug problems, he was replaced with Roger McDowell, who was a starting pitcher for the New York Mets (1985-89).

This episode was originally titled "The New Friend" when it first aired.

This episode is sometimes referred to as "Of Mastodons and Men" but that title wasn't used or recognized by "Seinfeld" writers or producers.

In the series' history, this is the only time the episode title is featured in the opening credits.

The script timed out at forty-five minutes but the creators did not want to cut it any of it so they asked NBC for permission to do a one-hour episode.

In this episode, Jerry demonstrates the "magic loogie" on Newman as a parody of the movie *JFK* (1991). In the movie, Kevin Costner demonstrates the "magic bullet" on Wayne Knight.

Jerry's line, "And you want to be my latex salesman," was ad-libbed.

An alternate ending to the final scene was shot in which George thanks the tall woman for finding his wallet, then shows her the door.

This is one of Jerry Seinfeld's top-five favorite episodes.

36. "The Limo" (2.26.92)
Suzanne Snyder, the sexy Nazi Eva, returned to the series in season five, playing restauranteur Poppie's daughter (Audrey) in "The Pie" (ep 79).

37. "The Good Samaritan" (3.4.92)
One story line involves Kramer having seizures every time he hears Mary Hart's voice. Michael Richards initially objected to the storyline. According to Richards, "When I read the script, I thought, no way – this is too far out." However, he changed his mind after realizing it was based on an actual case reported in 1991 by the *New England Journal of Medicine*. Apparently, Hart's voice triggered abnormal electrical charges in Dianne Neale's brain causing epileptic seizures. "Entertainment Tonight" declined to lend its theme song for use in this episode.

In 2009 an Iowa man was fired from his job for sexual harassment, partially stemming from his use of the phrase "You are so good looking."

Ann Talman (Robin) received the role because she was dating Michael

Richards at the time. She also appears in an uncredited role in "The Trip, Part 1" (ep 41).

Jason Alexander's friendship with Helen Slater led to her agreeing to appear as Becky Gelke. She was chosen for the role because of her love for Superman, like Jerry Seinfeld, and for starring in the superhero movie *Supergirl* (1984).

Jason Alexander directed this episode. He is the first and only cast member to direct a "Seinfeld" episode.

38.　"The Letter" (3.25.92)

The Elaine story was inspired by a real-life experience. Larry David asked executive producer Howard West if he knew anyone who could get him tickets for a Yankees-Angels game at Anaheim Stadium. West knew the accountant of Angels owner Gene Autry and was able to get David seats in Autry's box behind the dugout. David, a New York native, wore a Yankees cap to game. An Angels executive came down to the box and asked David to remove the cap because it might offend Mr. Autry. David could be seen wearing the hat on the front page of the *Los Angeles Times* sports section the following day. The character "Leonard West" was named after "Howard West."

The portrait of Kramer entitled "The Kramer" became a popular poster and successful "Seinfeld" merchandising product. The portrait became available to purchase as a print within a few months of the episode's debut. The print sold for 20 dollars to a range of customers from college-aged consumers to mainstream adults who would hang it above their mantle.

After being hit in the head by a baseball, Kramer refers to Elaine as "Carol" and to George as "Mike." This is a reference to Carol Leifer (basis for Elaine's character) and Michael Costanza (Seinfeld's friend and basis for George's last name).

Phil Rizzuto lends his voice as the TV Announcer in this episode. He was a Hall of Fame shortstop for the New York Yankees (1941-56) and popular TV and radio announcer for 40 years (1957-96) known for exclaiming "Holy Cow!" when there was a great play. He provided the baseball play-by-play element in Meatloaf's "Paradise by the Dashboard Light" but was never told the sexual innuendo of the song before recording his portion.

39.   "The Parking Space" (4.22.92)

The story of a parking spot confrontation was inspired by a similar incident that happened to writer Greg Daniels' father.

The street scenes were filmed outdoors with the live studio audience seated in a large set of bleachers behind the camera crew. The audience had trouble hearing the dialogue because there was no sound system. As the day wore on, the filming extended into the evening, resulting in the darker lighting of the later scenes in the episode.

Michael Costanza, a friend of Jerry Seinfeld and the inspiration for George Costanza's name, appeared in this episode as a Truck Driver. In 1999 he sued Jerry Seinfeld and Larry David for $100 million for using his last name, claiming a violation of privacy and emotional distress. The case was dismissed.

40.   "The Keys" (5.6.92)

This was the first crossover episode where two competing networks worked together on a prime time show: "Seinfeld" (NBC) and "Murphy Brown" (CBS). Larry David and Jerry Seinfeld later appeared on Diane English's (creator of "Murphy Brown") new show "Love & War" as a thank you for the "Murphy Brown" scene. They were seen at the end of an episode considering proposed "Seinfeld" scripts by the "Love & War" characters, one of which had Kramer sleeping with Elaine.

Kramer's appearance on "Murphy Brown" (along with a cameo appearance by Candace Bergen) was supposed to be a secret until entertainment reporter Marilyn Beck broke the story weeks before it aired.

Jerry Seinfeld was amazed at the efficiency and smoothness of the "Murphy Brown" production team. According to Jerry, "Everybody knows what they're doing! Our show is kind of a jalopy. We herk and jerk along. It's kind of rough, you know, and we like that. We don't really want to improve it."

Jerry and his date pretend to hurry into his apartment to escape approaching murderers. His date counters, "I'm from Wichita," a reference to the fact that Wichita was once terrorized by one of the most notorious serial killers of the 20th century, the BTK Killer.

According to the audition sheets, Jerry's girlfriend in this episode is called Lisa.

David Blasucci has an uncredited role as the Hippie. He worked as a "Seinfeld" production assistant.

Though it aired as the season finale, "The Keys" was shot before "The Parking Space" (ep 39).

Season 4: 1992-1993

Season Regulars
Jerry Seinfeld (Jerry Seinfeld), Julia Louis-Dreyfus (Elaine Benes),
Michael Richards (Kramer), Jason Alexander (George Costanza)

41-42. "The Trip, Part 1 & 2" (8.12.92)

The scene where Kramer approaches Fred Savage in a coffee shop was
inspired by the real-life experience of writer Larry Charles. The aspiring
writer once cornered Richard Dreyfuss in an LA bookstore and pitched
a movie. According to Charles, "I was so excited I started to
hyperventilate. I said, 'Don't be scared of me.'"

Julia Louis-Dreyfus does not appear in this episode because she was on
maternity leave at the time of filming. She was written out of the first few
episodes of season four, providing only cameo appearances. It was
explained that she was on vacation in Europe with her
psychiatrist/boyfriend, Dr. Reston.

The scene in which the man breaks into the car was shot near the Bicycle
Shack on Ventura Place in Studio City, California, a short distance from
CBS Studio Center, the main studio for "Seinfeld."

Kramer is residing in the same Hollywood hotel that was used in *Pretty
Woman* (1990).

When Kramer is confronted by the police at his apartment, Larry David
and episode writer Larry Charles can be seen standing in the crowd
behind the officers, at the far right of the scene.

Marty Rackham appears as a police officer. Rackham would return to the
series in a recurring role as Jake Jarmel, a novelist who dates Elaine for
a short time.

Towanna King (Secretary) (voice) worked as the lead stand-in for Elaine in 1990, and has an uncredited role in "The Pick" (ep 53).

Ann Talman (Woman in Exercise Video) dated Michael Richards from 1992-93.

43.   "The Pitch" (9.16.92)

The primary storyline about Jerry and George co-creating the television show "Jerry" was a playful homage to the process Jerry Seinfeld and Larry David experienced when co-creating the show "Seinfeld." Naturally, NBC executives were concerned about the idea of creating a show within a show.

Starting with season four, Jason Alexander objected to changing "Seinfeld" from a character-driven comedy to a serialized sitcom about Jerry and George's NBC project. According to Alexander, "'Seinfeld' made its fame and fortune on doing things in life, the little things that happen to everybody, but now we're out on a limb. This isn't our show. But I've been wrong more than I've been right." This time he was wrong because "Seinfeld" won its only Emmy Award for Outstanding Comedy in season four.

The recurring character "Crazy" Joe Davola was named after Larry David's friend. The real Joe Davola is entertainment executive in Hollywood. He insisted on having a character named after him.

Julia Louis-Dreyfus has a minimal role in this episode because she was on maternity leave at the time of filming.

"Seinfeld" writer Steve Skrovan appears as the character Tommy.

This episode was originally aired as a one-hour special along with "The Ticket."

44.   "The Ticket" (9.16.92)

David Graf (Cop #2) is best remembered as Tackleberry in seven *Police Academy* movies.

Julia Louis-Dreyfus has a minimal role in this episode because she was on maternity leave at the time of filming.

This is Wayne Knight's favorite episode.

45.   "The Wallet" (9.23.92)

Elaine's boyfriend/psychiatrist Dr. Reston was actually called Dr. Jeweler in the earlier drafts of this episode.

Julia Louis-Dreyfus returns from maternity leave to appear in an entire episode. Jerry Seinfeld was very happy to return Elaine to the show. He told *US Magazine* that while Louis-Dreyfus was gone "all of us felt out of balance, like there was a flavor missing from the ice cream split."

46.   "The Watch" (9.30.92)

Jessica Lundy (Hostess) is best known for costarring (with Cynthia Stevenson) in the briefly successful sitcom "Hope & Gloria" (1995-96); she also appears in "The Bubble Boy" (ep 47).

Mimi Craven (Cynthia) was married to director Wes Craven (1982-87) and worked as a flight attendant for Delta Airlines.

47.   "The Bubble Boy" (10.7.92)

The "Moors/Moops" misprinted answer in a board game was based on an actual incident that occurred to "Seinfeld" staff writer Bill Masters while playing the "Jeopardy!" board game (9th Edition, 1972).

Jon Hayman (Donald, the Bubble Boy) was a "Seinfeld" staff writer who wrote the episode "The Movie"(ep 54) and worked as a program consultant.

This episode relies heavily on dark comedy in the portrayal of the bubble boy. Typically, media coverage of "bubble boys" who live in quarantine due to an immune deficiency try to gain audience sympathy. The writers flip the perception by having the "bubble boy" as a selfish, obnoxious jerk, unworthy of sympathy. Executive producer George Shapiro noted all the negative reaction from all the bubble boys and their family and friends.

48.   "The Cheever Letters" (10.28.92)

Novelist Jay McInerny wrote an appreciation of "Seinfeld" and cited this episode in particular: "Any prime-time television show in which somebody's father gets outed posthumously by John Cheever earns my undying admiration."

49.   "The Opera" (11.4.92)

Bill Saluga (Usher) is best known for one role originating in 1976 as an obnoxious little fellow named "Raymond J. Johnson, Jr." When addressed as "Johnson," he would launch into a tirade starting, "You doesn't has ta call me Johnson--you can call me RAY or you can call me JAY...."

50.   "The Virgin" (11.11.92)

The subplot where Jerry is offered a show by NBC is based upon his real-life experiences. In the episode, Jerry suggests a script idea where all the main characters are waiting for a table in a Chinese restaurant but the executives are not impressed. This is an inside joke because NBC balked at the idea when it was proposed by Jerry Seinfeld and Larry David in season two's "The Chinese Restaurant" (ep 16).

The story was co-written by the famed Farrelly brothers (Peter and Bobby) who are known for writing outrageous comedies, such as *The Three Stooges* (2012), *Shallow Hal* (2001), *Me, Myself & Irene* (2000), *There's Something About Mary* (1998) and *Dumb & Dumber* (1994).

Bob Balaban (who plays Russell Dalrymple) was supposed to appear in this scene but the role was written out due to a scheduling conflict. It was established in the episode that Russell had to deal with "a problem on the set of 'Blossom.'"

Marla the Virgin was played by Jane Leeves who is best known for her role in "Frasier" (1993-2004) as Daphne; she appears in four "Seinfeld" episodes.

Jackie Swanson ("Cheers" as Kelly) and Dedee Pfeiffer (Michelle's sister) auditioned for the role of Marla, the virgin.

To celebrate the show's fiftieth episode, a cake was prepared and eaten by the cast and crew during the pre-show dinner.

The night this episode aired, Kramer made a one-scene appearance on "Mad About You" where it was revealed that he sublet his apartment from Paul Reiser's character years earlier.

51. "The Contest" (11.18.92)

Larry David was involved in a similar contest with his friends, and won by the third week though it was very difficult. Kenny Kramer did not compete because he felt he would lose. David wrote the episode but was hesitant to tell Jerry Seinfeld fearing he may find it offensive. Many thought it would never air because of the content. Seinfeld decided it would be funnier to infer that George masturbated, rather than stating it outright. Part of the opening scene contains some of the script that was originally meant to be used in the original "Seinfeld" pilot (ep 1).

Despite the sensitive subject matter in the episode, NBC only received 21 complaints and no commercial advertisements were pulled.

Larry David thought NBC would reject the episode, and he was prepared to quit. He had the entire scenario worked out in his head.

Marla the Virgin (Jane Leeves) and Jerry (Jerry Seinfeld) listen to Elaine (Julia Louis-Dreyfus) discussing her sex life.

In the episode, Jerry sings "The Wheels on the Bus" (while watching Tiny Toon Adventures). In the original script he was watching "Flipper" but it was changed due to concerns over music rights.

A porno movie called *The Bet* was released soon after "The Contest" aired and became a subject of great amusement around the "Seinfeld" offices. Another porno called *Hindfeld* was made the following year.

There are two deleted scenes in "The Contest." One features Joyce, the teacher of Elaine's fitness class, in the opening scene talking to Elaine, Jerry and Kramer. The second features George and Estelle Costanza in the hospital, where the female patient has been moved to the room next-door after Estelle complained about her nakedness.

This is the first episode for the character Estelle Costanza. Estelle Harris never saw "Seinfeld" before her audition for the role. She was only in town for a brief while when the part of George's mother was first written. If not for this perfect timing, she would not have been considered, as the show was never known to fly in actors just for an audition. Harris turned out to be perfect for the part. The cast and crew thought she looked like Jason Alexander, which made it believable that their characters could be related. In fact, Alexander's real-life mother looks similar to Harris.

This is one of Jerry Seinfeld's top-five favorite episodes.

John F. Kennedy Jr. did not object to being named as a character in the episode. Although he did not personally appear in the show, his role was played by an actor who is not named in the credits.

After its acclaimed premiere, the first repeat airing of "The Contest" scored the highest Nielsen rating in the show's history: a 20.1 rating and a 30 share, compared to a 13.0/19 on its premiere.

52.   "The Airport" (11.25.92)

Due to the large number of sets, "The Airport" required shooting on a second soundstage, which was a first for the show. Shots inside the plane were filmed on the usual stage 19, while all scenes in the airport, such as Kramer sliding down the baggage chute, were shot on the auxiliary stage.

The shot of Kramer running alongside the airplane was filmed in the parking lot on the northern end of the CBS Studio Center Backlot.

There is an alternative ending that was never aired where George meets up with Elaine and Jerry at the baggage claim, beaten up, saying in a daze, "You won't believe what happened to me."

Jennifer Campbell, who plays fashion model Tia, jump started her acting career by winning the Miss Hawaiian Tropic International contest in 1989.

Mark Christopher Lawrence (Sky Cap) is best known as Big Mike in "Chuck" (2007-12); he also appears in "The Race" (ep 96).

In the airplane scene where Elaine is offered a kosher meal, the voice from across the aisle claiming that he ordered it is uttered by Larry David.

Episode writer Larry Charles has a cameo appearance as the man exiting the airplane bathroom before Elaine enters. She has to hold her breath before going into the restroom.

"Seinfeld" writer Bill Masters is the airport shuttle van driver who refuses to wait for Jerry and Elaine.

53.   "The Pick" (12.16.92)

The original episode title was "The Nipple" but Larry David thought it was too sexually explicit for network television executives.

George's long ascent to Susan's apartment was shot in the stairway of Building 5 at the CBS Studio Center. Building 5 housed the "Seinfeld" production and writing offices for seasons 2-9. This is the only episode scene to feature the inside of Building 5.

Gina Hecht (Dana) appears in three "Seinfeld" episodes; but may be remembered as Jean DaVinci in "Mork & Mindy" (1979-81). She introduced Pam Dawber to her future husband Mark Harmon.

54.   "The Movie" (1.6.93)

Steve Skrovan, the cowriter for this episode, has an uncredited part as Movie Patron; he is the man with the white hat seated next to Elaine.

Episode filming went on into the wee hours of the morning, with production wrapping at about 3:30 a.m.

Rochelle, Rochelle, the fictional movie Jerry spends the episode trying to see, returns to the series as a musical in "The Understudy" (ep 110).

55. "The Visa" (1.27.93)

Writer Larry Charles referred to "Seinfeld's" fourth season as its "Sergeant Pepper Year" because "the show went from "I Love Lucy" to Thomas Pychon, from Al Hirt to John Coltrane."

56. "The Shoes" (2.4.93)

In this episode there is a scene where Elaine complains that she is not included in the "Jerry" pilot script. Jerry replies that they can't write for a woman. This is a reference to the original "Seinfeld" pilot script that did not have a lead female character. NBC demanded a female character as a condition of picking up the series.

This was the first episode when "Seinfeld" was permanently switched to Thursday night after "Cheers," which commenced "Seinfeld's" permanent run as a top ten TV show. The creators were worried that the switch would result in many first-time viewers not understanding the story arc of the "Jerry" pilot.

According to Julia Louis-Dreyfus, one of the few scenes to make her squirm was her cleavage-related moment where she flaunts her breasts in front of Russell Dalrymple. She didn't mind talking about it, but showing it was a little less comfortable for her.

Denise Lee Richards is best known for her make-out scene with Neve Campbell in *Wild Things* (1998) and the highly-publicized divorce with Charlie Sheen in 2006. In this episode, she plays Russell Dalrymple's 15-year-old daughter with abundant cleavage; she was 22 years old at the time of filming.

57. "The Outing" (2.11.93)

This episode was created by Larry Charles based upon rumors about Jerry

Seinfeld's sexuality. The script idea was nearly abandoned over fears of offending the gay community. However, when Charles came up with the tag line "not that there's anything wrong with that" as a way of salvaging the episode, Seinfeld knew this would be socially acceptable. The purpose of the script idea was to satirize homophobia and excessive political correctness.

Larry Charles created the classic line "Not that there's anything wrong with that" after being told by Castle Rock executive Glenn Padnick that blatantly rejecting the idea of being called gay might appear insensitive. Repeating the line as often as possible was suggested by Jerry Seinfeld.

This was the first new episode of "Seinfeld" to air in its new permanent timeslot on Thursday nights after "Cheers." The move saw "Seinfeld's" audience increase by 57% and go from being the 40th most watched show straight to the top 10 in the Nielsen ratings.

58.   "The Old Man" (2.18.93)

Jerry's old man, Sidney Fields, is a reference to a man by the same name who was a writer and actor (as the landlord) in "The Abbott and Costello Show," which was a major influence in Jerry Seinfeld's comedy. The other old man was named Ben Cantwell, who was a pitcher for the Boston Braves, and in 1935 lost 25 games, the most ever in a single season.

In an alternate ending that was never broadcast, the housekeeper reveals that she speaks fluent English, with an accent native to New York, not Senegal, causing George to lose interest in her.

Tobin Bell (record store owner, Ron) is best known as Jigsaw/John Kramer in all the *Saw* movies.

Victoria Dillard, the agency rep, is most known as Janelle Cooper in "Spin City" (1996-2000) and being the former longtime girlfriend of Laurence Fishburne.

59.   "The Implant" (2.25.93)

Writer Peter Mehlman used personal experience for this episode. There was a man at his health club that actually looked like Salman Rushdie, and the double-dip experience happened at a party Mehlman attended.

Marc Hirschfeld noted that casting the role of Sidra was especially challenging: "We had to find not only attractive actresses that were funny but they had to be well endowed as well. In Hollywood, that's not much of a problem, but we had a number of actresses audition for the role and Teri Hatcher was not only exquisite but funny, had attitude, and was a slam dunk for that role."

Sidra's parting shot to Jerry at the end of this episode was scripted as simply "Oh, by the way, they're real." Teri Hatcher ad-libbed the kicker "and they're spectacular."

Teri Hatcher (Sidra) was a San Francisco 49ers cheerleader in 1984 and auditioned for the female lead role of Jamie Buchman in "Mad About You" (lost to Helen Hunt). She is best known for roles in "Desperate Housewives"and "Lois & Clark: The New Adventures of Superman." Hatcher's career started when she accompanied a friend to an open casting call for "The Love Boat;" she also auditioned and received a part as Amy the dancing mermaid that lasted 22 episodes (1985-86).

Megan Mullally is most-recognized role as Karen Walker in "Will & Grace." She auditioned for the role of Elaine in "Seinfeld" and Grace in "Will & Grace."

The actor who plays Timmy, the boy who objects to George double-dipping a chip, is Kieran Mulroney, the younger brother of actor Dermot Mulroney.

While in the sauna set, Jerry and the gang held a brief, impromptu "towel fashion show" for the studio audience.

60.   "The Junior Mint" (3.18.93)

A Peppermint Pattie was used for filming the surgery scene because a Junior Mint was too small for the camera to detect.

Jerry ad libbed the phrase, "Let's go watch them cut this fat bastard up" and claims this scene opened the door for the characters to become darker and edgier in subsequent episodes.

In Wisconsin, Jerold Mackenzie, a Miller Brewing Company executive, was fired for "poor managerial judgment" after recounting the scene where Jerry tried to remember a girlfriend's name that rhymed with a part of the female anatomy. A female secretary complained it was sexual harassment when he copied a page of the dictionary that had the word clitoris. Mackenzie filed a lawsuit for wrongful termination and won. The jury awarded $26.6 million but the decision was overturned on appeal for issues unrelated to the "Seinfeld" episode.

61. "The Smelly Car" (4.15.93)

The episode idea came from Peter Mehlman's lawyer friend who was complaining about the ordeal of not being able to get the smell out of a car. Of all the bad ideas pitched by Mehlman's friend, he finally struck gold.

Michael Des Barres, the restaurateur forced to sit inside the smelly car, is best remembered as Murdoc in "MacGyver." He is also an accomplished singer and musician; he was the lead singer of Power Station when Robert Plant was unable to tour in 1985 and after Freddie Mercury's death, Des Barres rejected an offer to be the frontman of Queen.

The car thief is played by Grant Heslov. He and George Clooney founded the production company Smoke House. In 1982 Heslov loaned Clooney $200 to buy his first set of headshots, and they have been friends ever since (and later writing and producing partners).

62. "The Handicap Spot" (5.13.93)

Executive producer George Shapiro noted minor controversy surrounding this episode: "We got some negative letters, but, we did get a letter from a handicapped group that complimented the show for treating the person with intelligence and humanity."

Kramer being rejected by a handicapped woman because he was a "hipster doofus" was inspired by an article in the December 1992 issue of *Atlantic Monthly* where writer Francis Davis' use of the description caught the attention of Larry David who then incorporated it into the script.

The episode originally had actor John Randolph portraying Frank Costanza but he was replaced by Jerry Stiller. When the series went into syndication the Randolph scenes were reshot with Stiller.

Kramer makes a reference to "make sure we don't forget where the car's parked" as a reference to "The Parking Garage" (ep 23) where the entire episode involves the gang search for their car in a mall parking ramp.

Kathy Kinney, a member of the mob that vandalizes Frank Costanza's car at the mall, is best known as Mimi in "The Drew Carey Show."

Beginning in March of 1993, "Seinfeld" became the first show to improve on the Nielsen ratings of its "Cheers" lead-in since "Taxi" did it a decade earlier.

63.   "The Pilot, Part 1" (5.20.93)

Larry Hankin, the actor who plays Kramer in the "Jerry" sitcom, actually auditioned for the role of Kramer on "Seinfeld" and was Larry David's first choice because he acted most like Kenny Kramer, the inspiration for the character.

"Seinfeld" writer Steve Skrovan has an uncredited role as Man in Restaurant.

Though written, filmed and originally broadcast as a one-hour season finale, "The Pilot" was split into two halves for syndication. This two-part episode aired in full prior to the series finale of "Cheers" and resulted in its largest viewing audience to date with 32 million viewers, according to the Nielsen ratings.

64.   "The Pilot, Part 2" (5.20.93)

During the scene where Russell is at sea, fellow shipmates include "Seinfeld" creator Larry David and writer Larry Charles.

Warren Littlefield, the president of NBC at the time, appears in this episode.

Rick Ludwin was the NBC executive who recruited Jerry Seinfeld to star in a show.

This episode has numerous "Seinfeld" employees appearing on camera: Shirley Beck (hair stylist), Elza Camacho (boom operator), Tom Cherones (director), Victor Wayne Harris (assistant property master), Darin Henry (writer), Janet Kagen (script supervisor), Dennis Kirkpatrick (boom operator), Pete G. Papanickolas (key grip), Pete San Filipo Sr. (sound mixer), and Jeffrey Yerkes (assistant writer).

Season 5: 1993-1994

Season Regulars
Jerry Seinfeld (Jerry Seinfeld), Julia Louis-Dreyfus (Elaine Benes), Michael Richards (Kramer), Jason Alexander (George Costanza)

65. "The Mango" (9.16.93)

The original title of this episode was "The Orgasm" but the creators thought the title was too risque for NBC executives.

One of Larry David's friends came up with the idea for Elaine to claim she never had an orgasm with Jerry. David thought this concept was too good to pass up. The subplot of Kramer being banned from a fruit shop is based on Larry David's personal experiences where he was banned from a fruit shop for squeezing the produce too much.

The exterior shot of Joe's fruit shop is not in New York, but is actually on the backlot of CBS Studio center.

The name "Almo's Bar and Grill" can be spotted on the storefront next to Joe's fruit stand. This is a reference to"Seinfeld" set designer Tom Azzari's father, Almo.

Larry David used the pseudonym "Buck Dancer" for his writing credit in the episode. It was corrected on the DVD collection.

Jerry Seinfeld appears in several scenes wearing a "Queens College" t-shirt to commemorate his alma mater.

Lisa Edelstein (George's girlfriend Karen) is best known as Dr. Lisa Cuddy in "House."

66. "The Puffy Shirt" (9.23.93)

This is the first appearance of Jerry Stiller as Frank Costanza. Prior scenes with John Randolph were reshot when the series went into syndication.

Following this episode's airing, Jerry started being heckled in his real stand-up appearances with pirate comments yelling "Avast ye matey!"

Jerry flew to New York to film his "Today Show" appearance with Bryant Gumbel on the show's actual set.

The Puffy Shirt was put on display at the Smithsonian National Museum of American History in 2006.

This episode is one of Larry David's all-time favorites.

67. "The Glasses" (9.30.93)

The glasses story was inspired by writer Tom Gammill's real experience of having his glasses stolen while changing clothes in a locker room.

The exterior of the Health Club was actually the same building which housed the cast's dressing rooms during the time "Seinfeld" was shot on Stage 19.

While trying to stop the air conditioner from falling out of Jerry's apartment window, Michael Richards nearly broke his ribs. After the episode finished filming, he was taken to the hospital for precautionary x-rays.

In the scene where Jerry tries to discover his girlfriend's infidelity, he devises a plan ending in "It's Howdy Doody time." Kramer then replies, "Right this way, Mr. Doody," which is a line made popular by Larry David on the short-lived TV show "Fridays" (with Michael Richards).

The jokes about George being able to see when he squints were added by Larry David and Jerry Seinfeld in script revisions made during production.

Rance Howard (Blind Man) is the father of accomplished actor/director Ron Howard and actor Clint Howard. He also appeared in "The Bottle

Deposit" (ep 132).

68.   "The Sniffing Accountant" (10.7.93)

In real life, Jerry Seinfeld's accountant stole approximately $50,000 to buy illegal drugs, thus inspiring the main plotline for this episode. Thereafter Jerry used his sister Carolyn as his financial manager.

In the 1970s Larry David worked as a bra salesman to support his struggling career as a comedian. A writer's assistants called bra companies to research the configuration of modern bras so David could write appropriate dialogue.

Larry David performed research for the recurring pick-up technique of using the index finger and thumb to feel the shirt sleeve of another person. David wanted to assess the different kinds of material and individual reactions.

Kramer's display of simultaneous drinking and smoking in this episode was unscripted, and required two takes to get right. After the first attempt, Michael Richards let out a loud belch (with smoke) that necessitated a second try at the scene.

The stake out scene was special to Wayne Knight because he worked as a private investigator for five years. In New York, after his Broadway stint, Knight needed work but did not want to be a waiter so a friend hired him because he liked to hire actors for that line of work.

The audience makes their final spontaneous applause for Kramer's entrance in this episode. The response was nixed by Larry David, who thought it ruined the reality and stole precious seconds away from the show. The audience warm-up comedian would tell the crowd in advance to resist the urge to clap during Kramer's entrances.

This was the first "Seinfeld" episode filmed on Stage 9 at CBS Studio Center in Studio City, California. The significantly larger stage allowed an expanding storyline for the "Seinfeld" production crew. "Seinfeld" remained on Stage 9 throughout the rest of the series.

Christa Miller (Ellen, the company owner who's garment is fondled by George) also appeared as "Cougar Town," "Scrubs," and "The Drew

Carey Show." She also appears in "The Doodle" (ep 106) and was on the cover of the first issue of *Maxim* magazine. Her husband, Bill Lawrence, created "Scrubs."

This is also one of Michael Richards' favorite episodes.

69.   "The Bris" (10.14.93)

The incident of discovering a pigman in a hospital bed parodies the British film *O Lucky Man!* (1973) where Malcolm McDowell discovers a half man/half pig in a hospital.

Jason Alexander wishes he never made this episode; he objected to the mohel's disdain for children.

The hospital sets were re-used several more times in the series. This was possible because production company Castle Rock took the unusual step of renting a warehouse to store old sets, instead of having them built to order. This allowed the costs to stay relatively low and made it possible to shoot episodes with as many as twenty sets.

The Pig Man's squeals and snorts were provided by "Seinfeld" production worker Brady Thomas.

70.   "The Lip Reader" (10.28.93)

Monica Seles was approached to appear in the final scene where Kramer runs into her on the tennis court. Seles turned down the offer and a stuntwoman was used instead and shot from behind.

Larry David and former writer Steve Skrovan provided the commentary for the US Open TV coverage which shows George devouring a sundae. David also provides the voice of the dispatching clerk for the car service company.

The "Seinfeld" staff had a few uncredited appearances: Jeff Bye (Man at Shop) worked as a production assistant and audience warm-up comic; Marc Hirschfeld (Tennis Crowd) worked as the casting executive; and Brian Myers (Tennis Crowd) was the casting associate director.

71. "The Nonfat Yogurt" (11.4.93)

This episode was scheduled to be aired two days after the New York City mayoral election so the production crew produced two different endings: one with David Dinkins winning, and another with Rudolph W. Giuliani winning. The cast recorded a line mentioning Giuliani, followed by the same line using the name Dinkins. Giuliani won the election so his segment was filmed on the morning after his victory. Dinkins refused to appear if he won the election so the creators already hired Phil Morris (subsequently cast as attorney Jackie Chiles) to play Dinkins' press secretary and taped a segment. Both versions of the episode are included on the Season Five DVD.

The opening monologue about wearing glasses as a newborn baby was made up of ad-libbed quips Jerry made to the audience. Coincidentally, a line in the episode has Jerry bragging about improvising ten minutes of comedy about the origins of the Ottoman Empire.

Though it aired before "The Barber," this episode was actually filmed two weeks later. As a result, the effects of Jerry's bad haircut can be seen before he even received it.

All curse words spoken were in fact words that just sounded like swear words. Thus, by bleeping the words, technically all swearing was simply inferred, thereby avoiding any regulatory violations.

The name Lloyd Braun was inspired by a Hollywood executive and friend of Larry David whose real name is Lloyd Braun.

The character Lloyd Braun is played by Peter Keleghan who was subsequently replaced by actor Matt McCoy.

Jerry Stiller recalls that after hitting George on the head in this episode, Estelle Harris asked if she could hit him too. She was told by Larry David that only one person can hit George per show.

72. "The Barber" (11.11.93)

The storyline of Kramer appearing in a celebrity bachelor auction was a late replacement for another story involving Elaine enlisting Kramer to help her get an antique barber chair for her apartment.

The classical music in "The Barber" was added as an afterthought when Larry David thought the episode needed something different to keep up the energy in the hair cutting story.

"Seinfeld" best boy grip David Richardson appears in this episode as a happy customer of Gino.

"Seinfeld" writers Tom Gammill & Max Pross appear in this episode as office workers. They have been a writing team since their days at Harvard.

73.   "The Masseuse" (11.18.93)

In the episode Elaine is dating Joel Rifkin who also shares the same name of a serial killer in New York. She suggests changing his name to OJ who coincidentally the following year was charged with killing his ex-wife and her friend.

Jennifer Coolidge (Jerry's masseuse/girlfriend Jodi) is best remembered as Sophie in "2 Broke Girls," Stifler's Mom in the *American Pie* movies, and Paulette in the *Legally Blonde* franchise; "Seinfeld" was her first acting job. Coolidge is listed as 5'10" tall and was considered for the role of Lynette Scavo in "Desperate Housewives."

Real New York Giants stadium announcer Bob Sheppard provided the voice-over announcements calling for Joel Rifkin to report to the stadium office.

74.   "The Cigar Store Indian" (12.9.93)

Gus's Smoke Shop, where Kramer tries to sell the cigar store Indian, is the name of the real cigar store where the "Seinfeld" writing staff would often buy their Cuban cigars. The exterior of the real shop is visible in the establishing shot of the episode.

Writers Tom Gammill and Larry David both provided voice-overs for subway announcers who says "Next Stop: Queensborough Plaza."

Sam Lloyd reprises the role of Ricky in "The Pie" (ep 79). Lloyd is best known as Ted, the hapless loser and hospital attorney, in "Scrubs."

Al Roker of NBC's "Today Show" flew from New York for a brief appearance in this episode. Roker, like Jerry Seinfeld, is an alumnus of Queens College.

75. "The Conversion" (12.16.93)

Episode writer Bruce Kirschbaum was unaware that the Latvian Orthodox church existed when writing the script. He originally intended to have a fictitious sect. Kirschbaum received many thank you letters from the church for bringing attention to the denomination.

The shots of Kramer running up the subway steps and into the streets of New York are not actually shots of Michael Richards. For several episodes, a body double was hired, dressed in Kramer's clothes and asked to run through the streets. This is obvious because each scene only shows Kramer running from behind.

When Kramer opens his apartment door for Jerry, the interior contains a real-life Jerry Seinfeld acting headshot framed and mounted on the wall.

Kramer (Michael Richards) wears garlic to be less alluring to the opposite sex in "The Conversion."

76.   "The Stall" (1.6.94)

All the rock climbing scenes were filmed on Stage 9. A thirty foot "rock" was built to hold the actors as they scaled the surface. The illusion was completed through the use of blue screen effects which showed sky and clouds behind the actors.

In this episode, Kramer refers to George as a "ginga," the first of many made-up words Michael Richards used for Kramerisms in the show's later years.

77.   "The Dinner Party" (2.3.94)

The Middle Eastern actor who played "Saddam Hussein" had a thick accent and his lines were deemed incomprehensible. His voice was dubbed over by Larry David using a bad British accent. "Hussein" originally asked Kramer and George for directions.

When George and Kramer are in the liquor store there are posters advertising beer for sale. By law, liquor stores in New York State are allowed to sell liquor, wine and lottery tickets and nothing else, including beer.

George and Kramer visit a newsstand that sells *Entertainment* magazine. The rack displays covers from five different issues. However, a newsstand only carries the most current issue of a magazine.

78.   "The Marine Biologist" (2.10.94)

Kramer hitting golf balls into the ocean is based on Larry David's practice of doing this while staying at a rented beach house the previous summer.

Jerry Seinfeld had the idea of having Kramer's golf ball getting stuck in the whale's blowhole.

It was originally planned to include a beached whale in the shot where George advances into the ocean to unclog the blowhole. After testing several different effects, it was decided that the scene worked fine without ever seeing the whale.

All the beach scenes were shot at the Will Rogers State Beach in Pacific

Palisades, California.

The audience response to the end of George's whale of a story is regarded by many as one of the longest sustained laughs by the "Seinfeld" studio audience in the show's history, rivaled only by the response to Kramer's line "I'm out" from "The Contest."

Larry David provides the voice of the person on the beach who asks, "Is anyone here a marine biologist?"

Jerry Seinfeld considers this to be one of his favorite episodes.

79. "The Pie" (2.17.94)

The incident of a female companion refusing pie by shaking her head but never saying a word to explain why was based upon an actual incident involving Jerry Seinfeld.

The Elaine mannequin was specially-made for this episode; a mold of Julia Louis-Dreyfus' face was made to keep the resemblance as close as possible.

George's suit did not make a swooshing sound. This was added in post-production.

Production was interrupted by the Northridge Earthquake on January 17, 1994. Due to the extensive structural damage to the set, the "Seinfeld" production team nearly moved the show to Paramount Studios. Unwilling to give up its most successful show, CBS Studio Center paid to have the damaged stage repaired in record time (three weeks), allowing "The Pie" to be completed and air exactly one month after the quake hit. As an additional incentive, CBS planned on renovating its New York Street backlot, which "Seinfeld" began using in season six.

80. "The Stand-In" (2.24.94)

Larry David noticed how many little people were working as stand-ins for children on sitcoms such as "Grace Under Fire" and "Roseanne" which inspired this episode. In his early days in Hollywood, Danny Woodburn worked as a stand-in for children.

Marc Hirschfeld recalls the difficulty in casting a little person who fit the show's comic sensibilities: "The frustration of the job was that we would get a script which would describe the fact we needed a funny little person who was a major guest role on the show with absolutely no advance notice from the producers. I remember we were doing two shifts. Brian Myers was pre-reading actors in one room and keeping the actors he thought were funny enough and then I was in the second room with Jerry and Larry auditioning the actors who Brian thought deserved a second look. We had Danny Woodburn come in and he was terrific and so, so funny and once again with a voice that was so distinctive that the guys just fell in love with it."

"The Stand-In" is the only "Seinfeld" episode to show any of the cast actually riding a New York City public bus.

81.   "The Wife" (3.17.94)

The actress playing Jerry's French "mistress" did not actually speak with a French accent. The decision to change her nationality was made after production and a voice-over actress was hired to loop all the character's speeches with the new accent.

Courteney Cox (Meryl) is best remembered in "Friends," "Cougar Town," and the *Scream* franchise. Many people remember Cox as the "surprised" girl who is pulled onstage by Bruce Springsteen in the music video "Dancing in the Dark" in 1984. She was paid $350 for this role. Although unknown at the time, Cox was an established model who appeared on numerous romance novel covers. She was offered the role of Rachel on "Friends" but preferred the character Monica.

82.   "The Raincoats, Part 1" (4.28.94)

The jacket George wears in the beginning of "The Raincoats" is the same one that was given by the producers to the cast and crew for a Christmas gift the previous year.

The final shot of the episode involving Rudy burning Frank Costanza's cabana clothes was filmed in the alley outside the show's writer's office. Rudy's line, "Lousy, moth-ridden crap," was actually added by Larry

David during post-production.

This episode originally aired as a one-hour special episode, paired with "The Raincoats, Part 2"

83. "The Raincoats, Part 2" (4.28.94)

References to the movie *Schindler's List* were included after Jerry Seinfeld discovered that Steven Spielberg was so depressed while filming the movie that he watched "Seinfeld" episodes to cheer himself up. The scene where Jerry and Rachel are making out during *Schindler's List* was added for Spielberg's benefit, and the final scene where Aaron claims he could have done more to get the Seinfelds to Paris is a parody of the movie ending.

The moths that tickle Kramer and flutter from his jacket were added to the scene in post-production and arranged according to where Michael Richards was looking during his performance.

The scenes outside a Paris cafe were shot in front of the CBS Studio Center commissary that was one building over from the "Seinfeld" production offices.

This is the first episode where someone other than Jerry says, "Hello, Newman." In this case, Helen Seinfeld says it in the same contemptuous tone.

84. "The Fire" (5.5.94)

The story of Toby's pinky toe injury was inspired by the tragic death of a friend's baby which resulted in her coworker's becoming jealous of the attention she received.

George's storyline started with one simple word: cowardice. The fire at a child's party was used to illustrate that point.

In the scene where Kramer describes his adventures on the bus while rescuing the pinky toe, it was originally intended to be filmed and shown over Kramer's description. The bus was rented and a crew was scheduled to stage the complete escapade but the success of Michael Richards' delivery of the story in front of the audience led the producers to keep things simple and stick with what obviously worked.

The alley scene shown after the fire was located directly behind the writers' office building. It was also the setting for future physical attacks on Kramer in later seasons.

Melanie Chartoff (Robin) was a regular with Larry David and Michael Richards in "Fridays" (1980-82), a short-lived series created to rival "Saturday Night Live."

Jon Favreau, an accomplished actor, director, writer and producer, plays the part of Eric the Clown.

Larry David provides the voice that announces Jerry's name before he goes on stage.

85.   "The Hamptons" (5.12.94)

The original working title for this episode was "The Ugly Baby."

The Hamptons beach house was actually a set shot and lit on the Seinfeld soundstage. A cyclorama of a marina was dropped behind the house to help insure an authentic look.

86.   "The Opposite" (5.19.94)

When George approaches a woman (Victoria) at Monk's Diner and proclaims, "My name is George. I'm unemployed and I live with my parents," the actress is Dedee Pfeiffer, the younger sister of famous actress Michelle.

Kathie Lee Gifford and Regis Philbin have cameo appearances and receive $75 royalty checks every time the episode is aired in syndication. Jerry Seinfeld found "Live with Regis and Kathie Lee" to be a fascinating show because "They're not doing anything. You can't do less than they do and make a living. And I for one couldn't be more impressed – to do little more than dent a seat cushion in a chair and make a zillion dollars." After seeing the "Live" hosts lovingly discuss a "Seinfeld" episode, Jerry, Julia and Michael filmed a parody and sent it to the "Live" production office.

The unscripted spoof was broadcast on "Live" a few days later.

"The Opposite" marks the debut "appearance" of George Steinbrenner. Larry David provided the voice of the Yankees owner.

Season 6: 1994-1995

Season Regulars
Jerry Seinfeld (Jerry Seinfeld), Julia Louis-Dreyfus (Elaine Benes),
Michael Richards (Cosmo Kramer), Jason Alexander (George Costanza)

87.   "The Chaperone" (9.22.94)

Elaine interviews for an editor position with Doubleday to replace
Jacqueline Kennedy Onassis. This reference paid homage to the former
first lady who died on the airing date of the season 5 finale; she worked
as an editor for Doubleday since her husband Aristotle Onassis' death in
1975.

The name "Mr. Pitt" was a late substitution for the name "Maurice
Templesman." Templesman, a mysterious millionaire diamond merchant,
was the last love of Jackie Onassis. Templesman refused use of his name
so the character was changed to Justin Pitt. Despite the change, Elaine
still won the character's attention because she happened to be dressed like
Jackie Onassis.

The Yankees' locker room scenes were actually shot inside the Anaheim
Angels' locker room when the Yankees were playing the Angels; these
scenes were scheduled and shot weeks in advance of the show's other
scenes.

Danny Tartabull was an outfielder for the New York Yankees from 1992-
95 and also appeared in "The Pledge Drive" (ep 89). Buck Showalter was
the New York Yankees manager from 1992-95.

Bob Sheppard, the stadium announcer's voice, was a legendary public
address announcer and the "voice" of Yankees Stadium since 1951 and
New York Giants since 1956. After delivering a tribute to Babe Ruth in
1948, the Yankees offered him a job on the spot. Sheppard did not accept

it until three years later when they guaranteed him an understudy for weekday games so announcing would not interfere with his job as a New York City speech teacher. He died in 2010 (age 99) and his microphone is enshrined in the Baseball Hall of Fame in Cooperstown, NY.

Renee Tenison, who plays a Miss America Contestant, is best known as *Playboy's* Playmate of the Month (November 1989) and Playmate of the Year (1990).

This is Andy Ackerman's directorial debut for the series; he became the primary director, replacing Tom Cherones.

Though he did not receive on-screen credit, Regis Philbin performed the voice-over for the Miss America emcee.

88.   "The Big Salad" (9.29.94)
The plot idea was based upon an incident that happened to Larry David. He once paid for someone's salad and the recipient thanked someone else.

This episode debuts a new exterior set for the New York street scenes. The exteriors were formerly shot on a collection of three small store fronts, but the new, more expensive street set allowed for new camera angles and framing opportunities.

89.   "The Pledge Drive" (10.6.94)
The voice of Dan, the high-talker, was originally performed by Brian Reddy speaking in a higher register but Larry David thought it still wasn't feminine enough so an uncredited woman was hired to perform the lines as a voice-over (which is why Dan's lips don't always synchronize perfectly with the sound of his voice).

The gas station scene in which George confronts the man who gave him the finger was actually shot at the CBS Studio Center's gas station and car wash.

Lisa Guerrero has an uncredited role as the PBS Telethon Producer. She may be recognized as a sideline reporter for MNF (2003) or being featured in the video game Madden NFL 2006. Guerrero worked as the entertainment director for three NFL teams, and posed for *Playboy* (January 2006).

90. "The Chinese Woman" (10.13.94)

After learning his parents are divorcing, George turns on the oven and puts his head inside. An alternate version had him pouring a bottle of water over his head.

Larry David makes his biggest onscreen appearance of the series as Frank Costanza's cape-wearing lawyer. The unnamed character also prevents Elaine's suicidal friend (Noreen) from jumping off a bridge.

91. "The Couch" (10.27.94)

Kramer and Poppie argue over when a pizza becomes a pizza, i.e., when you start making it or after if comes out of the oven. This is a metaphorical argument about the abortion issue, whether life begins at conception or birth.

The exterior shot of the convalescent home where Kramer visits Poppie while he recovers from his gastrointestinal maladies is actually Building 5 on the CBS Studio Center lot. This is the building which housed the "Seinfeld" production and writers' offices.

The moving truck company is "Azzari Movers" which is a reference to set designer Tom "Tho E" Azzari.

92. "The Gymnast" (11.3.94)

On this night of television programming, NBC promoted a blackout and urged its sitcom writers to pen an episode about a New York City blackout. While "Friends," "Mad About You," and "Madman of the People" all complied, Larry David refused to succumb to this advertising ploy and "Seinfeld" became the only series without a blackout-themed episode.

Clowns from Cirque du Soleil appear as extras in the circus scenes.

The long distance shots of Misha walking the high-wire were performed by a New York acrobat. A stunt double was instructed to fall during the close-up shot but instead the crew used actor Maurice Godin to perform the fall from a much lower height.

93.   "The Soup" (11.10.94)

In the closing scene George is eating at Reggie's Diner. He returns in "The Pool Guy" (ep 118), when his "worlds are colliding." Reggie's is later revealed to be the Bizarro Monk's in "The Bizarro Jerry" (ep 137).

Kenny Bania was called Alvin Bania in the original draft of "The Soup."

94.   "The Mom & Pop Store" (11.17.94)

The subplot involving Jon Voight's car was inspired by events that actually happened to writer Tom Gammill. He purchased a car purely based on the belief that it had previously been owned by Jon Voight, only to find out later that he had been lied to–it was owned by Jon Voight's mother. Gammill kept the car, however, and it was used as George's car in this episode and "The Gum" (ep 120) where it burns.

This episode uses the movie *Midnight Cowboy* as a common theme: Jerry wears cowboy boots, George sings the theme song "Everybody's Talkin'" by Harry Nilsson, Jon Voight starred in the movie, and Jerry comforts Kramer during a nose bleed on the bus.

Original Dixieland music was created specifically for this episode.

Jerry's line, "But I don't wanna be a cowboy," is a direct reference to a similar line in "The Puffy Shirt," "But I don't wanna be a pirate."

95.   "The Secretary" (12.8.94)

This is the first episode where George Steinbrenner is impersonated (other than a silhouette); Larry David provides the voice while the audience views the actor Lee Bear from behind. Both roles are uncredited. Lee Bear appears in ten "Seinfeld" episodes, all uncredited; his only other acting role was Cutter's Bodyguard in *Clear and Present Danger* (1994).

As Jerry, Elaine and Kramer walk home from Barney's, there is a store front for "Kal's Signs" in honor of Jerry's father, Kal Seinfeld, who owned a sign business during Jerry's childhood.

96. "The Race" (12.15.94)

Jerry's famous line, "I chose not to run" is taken from the 1928 presidential race when Calvin Coolidge's only reason for not running for president of the United States was: "I choose not to run for President in 1928."

This episode utilizes Jerry's affection for Superman more than any other episode, including dating a woman named Lois. It also contains the only instance of the show breaking the fourth wall: Jerry turns and addresses the camera for the last line of the show, "Maybe I will, Lois. Maybe I will." This was a reference to the Superman TV series from the 1950s. Finally, the theme tune for *Superman: The Movie* was used as background music for the footrace that ended the episode.

In a deleted scene, George explains being sent to Cuba and discusses with Jerry about not having a visa. When Kramer enters the apartment, George asks Kramer if he still knows people down at the Cuban Embassy. Kramer states that he plays golf with them, and the pair hurries to the embassy before it closes. By the time they arrive the building is closed. Kramer claims to know a secret passage that was built during the Cuban Missile Crisis. The next scene shows surprised Cubans when Kramer comes crashing down the chimney wearing a Santa Claus outfit.

97. "The Switch" (1.5.95)

The shots of Jerry talking on the phone to his girlfriend's roommate during his dream sequence were actually taken from a scene in "The Chaperone."

NBC invested a great deal of promotional time into this episode to hype the revealing of Kramer's first name after five and one-half years. The network was rewarded with the show's highest audience Nielsen rating to date.

Larry David provides the off-camera voice of the passerby who addresses Kramer on the street by saying "What do you say, Cosmo?"

98. "The Label Maker" (1.19.95)

George's sneeze just before Tim Whatley approaches on the street was unscripted. Though the director cut after the sneeze, it was edited into the final version to give the scene a more natural feel.

Though the exterior of Joe Robbie stadium is shown in stock footage, the interior where Jerry and Newman sit near the end of the episode was actually shot on bleachers temporarily installed on the production office parking lot.

Seinfeld's production accountant Eugene Lew is visible seated directly in front of Jerry in the show's last scene at the Super Bowl.

99. "The Scofflaw" (1.26.95)

Former Seinfeld writer Bob Shaw makes a brief appearance as a New York cabbie that pulls over to allow Elaine to chase after a man with

Elaine (Julia Louis-Dreyfus) taunts Jake Jarmel (Marty Rackham) by wearing identical glasses in "The Scofflaw."

attractive eyeglass frames. He returned to play the role later in the season in "The Understudy."

Daniel Benzali was originally scheduled to play the part of Officer Morgan but instead it was played by Ivory Ocean.

While Kramer is wearing his eye patch in this episode, he tells Jerry, "I want to be a pirate." This is, of course, a reference to Jerry's famous line from "The Puffy Shirt."

100-101. "Highlights of a Hundred, Part 1 & 2" (2.2.95)

102. "The Beard" (2.9.95)
Robert Mailhouse (Elaine's gay friend, Robert) plays drums in Keanu Reeves' band Dogstar.

"Seinfeld" writer Bruce Kirschbaum appears in the second police lineup.

It took several takes before Elaine was able to remove the toupee from George's head, and even more takes to throw the toupee out the window because Julia Louis-Dreyfus continually collapsed in a fit of laughter.

Larry David was the Seinfeld office's secret "Melrose Place" viewer.

103. "The Kiss Hello" (2.16.95)
Most of the apartment tenants' photos that Kramer hangs on the lobby wall are pictures of the "Seinfeld" production office staff.

Though it was technically the 103rd episode to air, "The Kiss Hello" was the 100th episode to be shot. The cast and crew were given commemorative jackets and sweatshirts to mark the occasion and a party was thrown after the show wrapped.

Wendie Malick (Elaine's physical therapy friend Wendy) is best remembered in "Hot in Cleveland," "Just Shoot Me," and "Dream On." In the 1970s, Malick worked in New York and Paris for five years as a Wilhelmina model and briefly in Washington, D.C. for Congressman

Jack Kemp. She also auditioned for the role of Diane Chambers in "Cheers."

The receptionist in this episode is played by Carol Leifer, a stand-up comedian who dated Jerry Seinfeld in the 1980s and became the inspiration for the character Elaine. In 2007 Leifer and her partner, Lori Wolf, adopted a son (Bruno).

104. "The Doorman" (2.23.95)

Following college, Larry David worked as a bra wholesaler which became the inspiration for George and Kramer (in a future episode) to dabble in the brassiere industry.

The doorman is played by Larry Miller, a well-recognized comedian and good friend of Jerry Seinfeld. He auditioned for the part of George Costanza.

At the end of the episode there is a scene where the German tourists chase Kramer down the street as he carries what they believe to be a stolen record player. They're calling out for someone to stop Kramer because they think he is a criminal. This scene is a parody of *The Marathon Man* (1976) where Laurence Olivier's character is recognized by New York Jewish immigrants as having been a Nazi torturer in a concentration camp during WWII. They follow him as he hurries along a New York City sidewalk and call for him to stop.

105. "The Jimmy" (3.16.95)

Mel Torme was not the first choice to appear in this episode. The part was originally written for Tony Bennett. Torme composed the music and words to "The Christmas Song" ("Chestnuts roasting on an open fire") with song writing partner Robert (Bob) Wells.

Torme's performance of "When You're Smiling" was filmed in one take resulting in one of the longest audience laughs in the show's history; the laughter volume had to be lowered to avoid drowning out the show's audio.

The episode writers anticipated hate mail after featuring a drooling, slurring Kramer being mistaken for a mentally-challenged man. The only response was from the mother of a mentally-challenged boy who indicated that her son loved the episode.

The women who appeared as Tim Whatley's dental hygienists were former *Playboy* playmates.

This episode marks the debut of George's boss, Mr .Wilhelm, who is portrayed by Richard Herd, who is often mistake for actor Karl Malden.

The paramedic, J.D. Bridges, is the older brother of Todd Bridges ("Diff'rent Strokes"). After college in the mid-80s, Bridges tried out as a free agent wide receiver with the LA Rams and Detroit Lions.

106. "The Doodle" (4.6.95)

When Jerry confronts Newman as the source of a flea infestation, there is a deleted scene where Newman frantically confesses that he was ambushed by a flea-infested bulldog named Buford. After the confession, Jerry smiles in delight before tossing the Chunky wrapper at the tortured postman.

Newman's apartment number is labeled 5F when it should be 5E.

George's doodling girlfriend Paula is played by Christa Miller who also appears in "The Sniffing Accountant" (ep 68) as Ellen.

The role of Elaine's publishing friend Judy is played by Coby Turner, who was a script supervisor for "Seinfeld" for several years.

107. "The Fusilli Jerry" (4.27.95)

Working titles for this episode included, "The Move," "The Proctologist," and "The Assman."

When casting "The Assman" (aka Dr. Cooperman), the casting directors were instructed to find an actor whose head looked like an ass.

Apollo Dukakis (Doctor) is the cousin of Massachusetts governor and 1988 presidential candidate Michael Dukakis, and brother of actress Olympia Dukakis.

108. "The Diplomats Club" (5.4.95)

Part of the subplot revolves around the fact that Tom Wright bears a striking resemblance to boxing legend Sugar Ray Leonard.

During the "Son of Sam" discussion, Newman mentions taking over the mail route for David Berkowitz, and indicates there were a lot of dogs on that route. Earl then asks if any of the dogs talked to Newman. Berkowitz (aka "Son of Sam") claimed that his landlord's "evil" dog commanded him to kill.

This episode featured the most sets of any half-hour episode of "Seinfeld," requiring two sound stages and multiple outdoor locations.

Jerry's manager Katie is played by Debra Jo Rupp who is best recognized as Kitty Foreman in "That '70s Show." After the first season, Rupp wore a wig because she suffered extensive hair damage from having her hair styled for every episode. She reprised the role of Katie in "The Abstinence" (ep 143).

Unable to find an actor with the right look for the pilot, the episode writers realized that the man who was delivering bottled water to the "Seinfeld" offices would be perfect. The delivery guy subsequently quit his job to become an actor.

109. "The Face Painter" (5.11.95)

Mark DeCarlo plays a character named Alec Berg, which is the name of one of the show's writers and executive producers.

The sentences spoken in Spanish by the priest but not translated via subtitles are: "The devil. My God. The devil." And the scene at the end: "The Madonna. Mother of Christ. I am not ready."

Writer and comedian Fred Stoller appears in an uncredited cameo as one of the fans behind the gang at the hockey game. Next to Stoller is Kenny Kramer, the inspiration for the character Cosmo Kramer.

The waitress who brings George his matzo ball soup is played by Peggy Lane, who worked for most of Seinfeld's nine seasons as a stand-in for Julia Louis-Dreyfus.

110. "The Understudy" (5.18.95)

The working title for this episode was "The Injury."

This episode is a parody of the 1994 Tonya Harding-Nancy Kerrigan scandal. The main plot involves an incident where the star is injured to give the backup an advantage. The final scene parodies the broken shoelace fiasco where the understudy asks to restart the program.

Actor Jack Luceno is the stunt double for Michael Richards when filming action scenes in New York City. He works gigs as a Kramer lookalike for corporate events, weddings, bar mitzvahs and other paid appearances.

Michael Richards' rendition of the *Beaches* theme song had to be dubbed in later because the star had difficulty remembering the tune on location.

Bette Midler is a famed singer and actress who started her musical career in 1970s by performing a cabaret act at the famed gay men's club, The Continental Baths, with Barry Manilow as her piano accompanist.

The day after the series was cancelled, John O'Hurley (J. Peterman) was hired to portray J. Peterman, the fictional catalogue clothier, at public appearances and offered co-ownership of the company to resurrect it from bankruptcy.

One of the women in Bette Midler's entourage is "Seinfeld" writer Marjorie Gross.

Both Jerry and George are seen playing baseball with their rights hands, even though they're left handed. The prop department did not have left-handed gloves.

Season 7: 1995-1996

Season Regulars
Jerry Seinfeld (Jerry Seinfeld), Julia Louis-Dreyfus (Elaine Benes), Michael Richards (Cosmo Kramer), Jason Alexander (George Costanza)

111. "The Engagement" (9.21.95)

Newman took over his mail route from "Son of Sam" (David Berkowitz). When Newman is arrested he says, "What took you so long?" to the police officer. This is the same sentence Berkowitz spoke when he was arrested for murder.

The scenes involving Julia Louis-Dreyfus shouting at the barking dog were filmed one day prior to shooting the rest of the show. She lost her voice performing the scenes so rather than postpone filming or dubbing her lines, the staff decided to write her laryngitis into the script, which is why Elaine has a hoarse voice throughout the entire episode.

The montage where George is reminiscing about the time spent with Susan was actually made up of scenes specially made for this episode. When George is standing on a pier, watching other couples, and thinking about marriage, the footage was filmed at the Santa Monica Pier.

The husband on the pier is "Seinfeld" producer Tim Kaiser. The woman on the pier is "Seinfeld" script supervisor Christine Nyhart.

"Happy, Pappy," the expression used by Susan that drives George to break up with her, is a real expression regularly used by the actress. After a performance, Heidi Swedberg would turn to Larry David and ask if it was a good take by saying, "Happy, Pappy?"

Mario Joyner appears in this episode because he is a good friend of Jerry Seinfeld. He also appears in "The Puerto Rican Day" (ep 176).

The man that Jerry is talking to as he is leaving the theatre after seeing *Firestorm* is Maroon Golf from "The Puerto Rican Day" (ep 176).

112. "The Postponement" (9.28.95)

While struggling to take his seat in the movie theater, Kramer actually injured the foot of the audience extra. She can be seen wincing in agony throughout the take.

Bruce Mahler appeared in three "Seinfeld" episodes as Rabbi Glickman and was a regular with Larry David and Michael Richards in sketch show "Fridays," where he also played a rabbi. He is best remembered as Douglas Fackler in four *Police Academy* movies. He took a break from acting to raise a family and breed champion border terriers.

113. "The Maestro" (10.5.95)

The subplot of Kramer suing over his coffee being too hot is based upon the infamous McDonald's coffee case.

The character Jackie Chiles was modeled after attorney Johnnie L. Cochran, Jr. who defended OJ Simpson in the double-murder trial. Phil Morris (the actor portraying Jackie Chiles) and Cochran visited the same LA barbershop for years so Morris was able to pickup Cochran's personality, habits and mannerisms. During the audition, Jerry Seinfeld had to turn up the air conditioning because Morris was so funny he was making Jerry sweat.

Ted Lange ("The Love Boat"), Michael Dorn (*Star Trek*) and Michael Boatman ("Spin City") auditioned for the part of Jackie Chiles.

Michael Richards' mispronunciation of the words "theater" and "cafè latte" was unscripted.

The Maestro's real name is Bob Cobb, which is the original alias of Mon-El, a supporting character in *Superman* comics.

Mark Metcalf (Maestro) is best remembered as Doug Neidermeyer in *Animal House* (1978). However, his claim to fame may be playing the father in the Twisted Sister video "We're Not Gonna Take It" using the sadistic, saliva-spraying ROTC Neidermeyer persona and saying the line, "You're all worthless and weak!" He also played a high school teacher in the Twister Sister video "I Wanna Rock."

Tim Bagley (Manager) once worked as a butler at the *Playboy* mansion and a phone service operator for two pimps.

When George is asking the security guard about having a chair, the same male extra in the background walks from right to left twice during the scene.

114. "The Wink" (10.12.95)

The promise to have Paul O'Neill hit 2 home runs was taken from the movie *Pride of the Yankees* (1942).

Elaine's line "Thanks for mutton" was ad-libbed by Julia Louis-Dreyfus on the day of shooting.

During the closing credits, Steinbrenner lists the many baseball managers he fired since becoming owner and accidentally mentions current manager Buck Showalter who would be fired soon after this episode was filmed.

115. "The Hot Tub" (10.19.95)

The scenes set at the starting and finishing lines of The New York City Marathon were actually filmed in a parking lot and road near the Griffith Park Zoo in Los Angeles.

When Elaine's neighbor Judy opens the door to discuss if she has seen Jean-Paul, the door nearly closes behind her and then suddenly opens wider without anyone visibly touching it. The door was not wide enough for the camera crew to film Elaine so the camera assistant had to widen the door himself to keep the take usable.

Scenes were shot for Larry the Cook (Lawrence Mandley) and Rabbi Glickman (Bruce Mahler) but deleted before the show aired.

The Houston Astros rep (Zeke) who calls everyone a bastard is played by Ernie Lively who is most recognized as Mr. Goodwrench in the TV commercials. He is also the father of actress Blake Lively ("Gossip Girl").

116. "The Soup Nazi" (11.2.95)

This was Spike Feresten's first writing credit for a "Seinfeld" episode. The idea arose when Feresten was a writer for "The Late Show with David Letterman" and staffers often discussed a local vendor they nicknamed "Soup Nazi." Feresten told Jerry Seinfeld and Larry David who immediately laughed and said, "That's a show. Do that as your first show." Feresten's inspiration for the armoire subplot was based upon his New York apartment building that had rules that forbade moving furniture on certain days. The armoire thieves were written as homosexual because Larry David decided that "only gay guys would steal an armoire."

The Soup Nazi was based upon real-life entrepreneur Al Yeganeh, who owned Al's Soup Kitchen International in New York. He also owns Original Soup Man, a national restaurant chain.

Jerry Seinfeld and several members of the production crew went to Soup Kitchen International for lunch weeks after "The Soup Nazi" aired. Upon recognizing Seinfeld, Yeganeh went into a profanity-filled rant about how the show had ruined his business and demanded an apology. Seinfeld gave "the most insincere, sarcastic apology ever given." Yeganeh parodied the episode by yelling, "No soup for you!" and ejected them from the restaurant. A tabloid even headlined that Yeganeh wanted to smack Jerry Seinfeld in the face because of the publicity.

Larry Thomas did not realize the character was based on a real person so he received inspiration for the part by watching *Lawrence of Arabia* and studying Omar Sharif's accent.

In the episode, Elaine imitates Al Pacino in *Scent of a Woman*. This was done at Jerry Seinfeld's suggestion, even though Louis-Dreyfus had never seen the film.

In the coffee shop scene where Jerry and George compete to see who can be the most affectionate, there is a deleted scene in which the manager approaches and asks them not to make-out in his shop. In the broadcast version, the manager can still be seen looking at them disapprovingly in the background as the two couples kiss. The scene was cut for time.

Alexandra Wentworth (Sheila, aka Schmoopy) met political correspondent George Stephanopoulos on a blind date; they married in 2001 and have two children. Her mother was the social secretary to First Lady Nancy Reagan and her father was a reporter for the *Washington Post*.

One of the customers ejected from the soup kitchen is played by Buddy Quaid, the half-brother of actors Dennis and Randy Quaid.

Like many Nazis (literal or figurative), the Soup Nazi flees to Argentina at the end of the episode.

The Soup Nazi's real name is not revealed until the series finale. His real name is Yev Kasem.

117. "The Secret Code" (11.9.95)

The firehouse shown is the Hook and Ladder #8 Firehouse in the Tribeca section of New York City. It was also used for exterior shots in both *Ghostbusters* films. The firehouse interior contains a *Ghostbusters* sign and photos taken with the cast and crew.

Lewis Arquette (Leapin' Larry) is the patriarch of well-known actor Rosanna, Patricia and David Arquette.

In an uncredited appearance, Seinfeld's dialogue coach Judy Kerr appears as the woman who approaches Jerry on the street after the fire. As dialogue coach, Kerr would work one-on-one with each cast member to help them learn their lines. She also appears in "The Abstinence."

Jerry reveals his ATM code to be "Jor-El," Superman's Kryptonian father. George's secret code is "Bosco," the name of the chocolate drink that his date once threw on him.

According to Elaine, her uncle worked at a book depository with Lee Harvey Oswald.

118. "The Pool Guy" (11.16.95)

Danny Hoch was originally cast as Ramon the Pool Guy but refused to use a Spanish accent because he felt the character would demean Latinos. Shooting the episode was postponed to cast a replacement. Hoch appeared in the Nas video "Be a Nigger Too."

Newman's one-piece, full-body bathing costume with cap was suggested by Wayne Knight; he thought the gag would be about the costume and not the fact that Newman was overweight.

George's meal at Reggie's Diner is re-used footage filmed for the final scene of "The Soup" episode. The same extra can be seen eating at the counter in both scenes.

Russ Leatherman, the real voice behind the Moviefone service, provides the voice of the man who stalks Kramer for stealing his business in the final scene of this episode.

"Seinfeld" writer David Mandel has an uncredited role as Man in Theater. He also wrote and co-directed (with "Seinfeld" writers Alec Berg and Jeff Schaffer) the hilarious movie *Eurotrip* (2004).

119. "The Sponge" (12.7.95)

The subplot of Kramer being bullied into wearing a ribbon is based upon the 1993 real-life controversy of former "Days of Our Lives" actress Deidre Hall who publicly refused to wear AIDS ribbons at public events, such as the Daytime Emmys. Hall claimed that the volunteers who passed out the ribbons bullied celebrities into wearing the ribbons.

There were several original storylines for this episode before it was settled on the one that aired:

1. Kramer and Newman buy stock in a company selling over-the-counter contraceptive devices to capitalize on the sponge being taken off the market. They go to Wall Street to start a buyout rumor on their company by whispering loudly about it at brokerage houses so the stock would go up 5-10 points before they sell. Kramer then shared his scheme with Elaine who immediately panics and buys as many sponges as possible. The plan backfires when Kramer and Newman fight with an obnoxious

guy in an elevator at Wall Street that starts a negative rumor about their company.

2. George meets a woman who argues that they are so alike that if they dated, they would have great sex for about ten days and then hate each other and split up. George ponders staying together for one week and then, by mutual consent, calling it quits. They get all the pleasure without the pain. Unfortunately, she only uses the Sponge contraceptive and Elaine cleared out the entire West Side.

3. Jerry's girlfriend asks if he donates to AIDS charities, and he admits donating to Kramer and Newman's company while touting its AIDS research. She decides to buy 5,000 shares right before the negative rumors are publicized and the stock price tumbles.

The alley scene featuring the AIDS charity walkers attacking Kramer was filmed directly behind the writers' office building. Other scenes were filmed in this location in future episodes, such as "The Foundation" where Kramer is attacked by his karate classmates.

120. "The Gum" (12.14.95)

The "Jon Voight" car is not shown moving in this episode because it was no longer operational (the engine had caught fire while being driven by its real owner, writer Tom Gammill). This accident inspired George's engine fire.

This is the first of only two credited appearances for Ruth Cohen (Monk's Diner Cashier) who appeared in 101 episodes.

Jerry's scenes while wearing the glasses in his apartment pay homage to screen comedian Jerry Lewis.

Larry David makes an uncredited cameo as a guy who sells George a pack of gum.

121. "The Rye" (1.4.96)

The exterior scenes were shot on the Paramount Studios lot. Filming went into the evening and a snowball fight broke out with the cast and crew.

The man in the Hansom Cab during the daytime tour is Eugene Lew who worked on "Seinfeld" as an accountant.

Jerry Seinfeld claims this is his favorite episode, especially the part where he steals the rye and runs down the street.

122. "The Caddy" (1.25.96)

The idea of using the trial to parody the OJ Simpson murder case was used when Kramer wanted Sue Ellen Mischke to try on the bra over her clothes. This is in reference to the prosecution having Simpson try on the bloody glove during the murder trial.

The exterior of the Yankee stadium offices where George parks his car is actually the exterior of the CBS Studio Center Administration building.

Brenda Strong (Sue Ellen Mischke) is best remembered as the narrative voice of Mary Alice Young in "Desperate Housewives." Strong was Miss Arizona in 1980 and a contestant in the 1981 Miss America pageant. She appears in four "Seinfeld" episodes.

When taping this episode, Brenda Strong had just given birth to a son, John Zakery Henri. She asked Larry David what size breasts he wanted because she could make them larger or smaller depending upon how often she nursed. He turned three shades of red before indicating that her breasts were fine the way they were.

Assistant Production Coordinator Jeff Bye played the uncredited role of Tom Cosley, Elaine's boyfriend in a flashback scene to high school. Julia Louis-Dreyfus actually dated a guy in high school by the same name.

123. "The Seven" (2.1.96)

The use of Newman being the judicious arbitrator is a direct reference to King Solomon's role in deciding the fate of a child.

Soccer star David Beckham and his wife Victoria (Spice Girls) named their fourth child Harper Seven.

Larry David named his first born after a player for the New York Knicks. Despite having a daughter, he named his child Cazzie after Knicks star

Cazzie Russell (1966-71).

Episode co-writer Alec Berg is the guy in the photo with Jerry's girlfriend Christie.

124. "The Cadillac, Part 1" (2.8.96)

This episode originally aired as the first half of a one-hour special along with "The Cadillac, Part 2." It was not originally planned as a double-sized episode, but after the show's first cut was completed Larry David realized that adding to the running time would be easier than making edits to shorten it to one-half hour. The sequence of Kramer running through the rooftops was added to fill the show out before broadcast.

One of the condo committee members (Ralph) was played by Jesse White. He is best remembered as the lonely Maytag repairman in TV commercials from 1967-88. White holds the distinction of being the first celebrity Jerry Seinfeld ever met. Jerry followed White several blocks to talk to the then-star.

125. "The Cadillac, Part 2" (2.8.96)

The final scene where Morty Seinfeld leaves the condo is a parody of President Richard M. Nixon's farewell. Just like Nixon, Morty Seinfeld slowly walks and waves to his supporters. The music from Oliver Stone's film *Nixon* (1995) was used for this scene.

The chase scene between Kramer and the cable guy is a parody of the movie *Vertigo* (1958).

When Kramer is chased by the Cable Guy, there is an obvious product placement of Rold Gold Pretzels that Kramer is eating out of his grocery bag. Not surprisingly, it was a product endorsed by Jason Alexander.

George is punched in the face by Marisa Tomei on the CBS Studio Center's then-brand-new Central Park set.

Marisa Tomei won an Oscar for Best Supporting Actress for her role in *My Cousin Vinny*. Not surprisingly, she was offered the part on

"Seinfeld" without auditioning.

126. "The Showerhead" (2.15.96)

This episode contains references to a Florida retirement community named Del Boca Vista. The name proved particularly difficult for Jerry Stiller to say, which resulted in several minutes of bloopers.

Kramer and Newman buying black market shower heads, all laid out on a cloth, is reminiscent of the movie *Taxi Driver* (1976) in which Travis Bickle (Robert De Niro) buys hand guns in the same fashion.

By the end of the show, when Elaine and Helen are trying to choose a cup for the urine sample, there is a reflection of a television and cameraman on the cupboard glass.

127. "The Doll" (2.22.96)

Stand-up comedian Kathy Griffin appears for the first time as Susan's college friend Sally Weaver. Soon after her appearance, Griffin appeared in an HBO comedy special in which she criticized Jerry Seinfeld for being rude to her during her time working on "The Doll." This inspired a storyline for "The Cartoon" (ep 169). Griffin was considered as a replacement cohost for "The View," and auditioned for the part of Phoebe on "Friends."

The working title for this episode was "The Doormat" because originally the doormat that George receives from Sally played a larger role in the episode plot; as the script was rewritten, the focus changed to Susan's doll collection and the episode was renamed accordingly.

Estelle Harris still owns the doll made of her likeness for this episode. The doll was constructed using a photograph of Harris shown only from the front so the sides of her face are not completely accurate.

In this episode John Lizzi plays the "The Other Guy" (Jose Carreras) who is the odd man out in the famous three tenors (the most notable are Luciano Pavarotti or Placido Dominguez). Lizzi once worked as a stand-in and photo double for Robert Blake and Charles Bronson.

The make-up lady is the "Seinfeld" make-up artist Patricia Messina.

Kramer's line,: "I've got a hunch, fat man. I can't lose" is taken from the movie *The Hustler* (1961) in a similar line delivered by Paul Newman to Jackie Gleason while playing billiards.

128. "The Friar's Club" (3.7.96)

The original title of this episode was "The Gypsies."

The Friar's Club is a private club whose members are mostly comedians and is well-known for risqué roasts of member and celebrities.

The Flying Karamazov Brothers appear as the Flying Sandos Brothers in this episode. The Karamazovs began as street performers in San Francisco in 1973.

Chalk camera marks are visible on the New York Street when George is nearly hit by the car at the beginning of this episode.

129. "The Wig Master" (4.4.96)

The Jiffy Park lot is also used in "The Muffin Tops" (ep 155) but it is named Jiffy Dump where Kramer wants to unload Elaine's muffin stumps. The episode also uses the same attendant and subtly acknowledges the unity of the two locations. At Jiffy Park the attendant tells Kramer that if he has a problem to take it up with Consumer Affairs. Thus, when denied access to Jiffy Dump by the same attendant, Kramer yells, "Maybe I will take it up with Consumer Affairs."

Larry David voices the cop who orders Kramer to turn to his right during his mug shot in the final scene.

130. "The Calzone" (4.25.96)

Paisano's Pizza is the name of a sub shop located in Studio City, near the "Seinfeld" offices, and a favorite lunch stop for the writers.

Danette Tays, who plays Jerry's irresistible girlfriend Nicki, appeared in a 1990s Rold Gold Pretzel commercial with Jason Alexander.

131. "The Bottle Deposit, Part 1" (5.2.96)

This episode originally aired as a one-hour special paired with "The Bottle Deposit, Part 2."

This bottle deposit storyline features the return of the original Kramer and Newman relationship which involved the two of them as schemers. After filming "The Old Man" (ep 58), Michael Richards complained that he was becoming a double act and requested that their relationship be played down considerably. Larry and Jerry decided to expand on Jerry and Newman's dislike of one another to keep the portly neighbor as a presence in the series.

Jerry's sensitive and highly protective mechanic Tony is played by Brad Garrett who is best remembered in "Everybody Loves Raymond" and "'Til Death." The 6' 8.5" actor had his first big break as a standup comedian by winning $100,000 on "Star Search" in 1984. He also appears on the ELO album "Discovery" on the back cover in a turban, wearing Middle Eastern clothing and holding a sword.

In 2007 a 15-person operation was busted for illegally smuggling millions of beverage containers from other states and cashing the deposit in Michigan. Police found over $500,000 in cash but unlike Kramer's scheme, the operation sold the cans to merchants at a discount, who then redeemed them for full value.

132. "The Bottle Deposit, Part 2" (5.2.96)

When Newman was running away, the farmer's daughter yells, "I love him. Goodbye, Norman, Goodbye" The creators thought the flubbed line was funny so they did not reshoot the scene.

At the end of the episode, Kramer and Newman dash through a cornfield to evade the farmer. After filming this scene, Wayne Knight experienced heart palpitations and was advised by his doctors to get into better shape. Knight credits this episode for motivating him to start a healthier lifestyle.

This episode was supposed to be 30 minutes but it was increased to an hour; however, the episode was only 41 minutes, not the typical 44 minutes for a one-hour sitcom episode.

The mail truck chase scene was filmed on the Pasadena Freeway in South Pasadena, California.

After discovering the farmhouse, Newman tells the farmer he was ambushed by survivalists. This is a reference to *The Postman* (1985) a novel by David Brin.

The farmer who chases Newman with his shotgun is played by Rance Howard who previously appeared as the Blind Man in "The Glasses" (ep 67).

133. "The Wait Out" (5.9.96)

Michael Richards injured his back filming the scene where his tight-fitting jeans are being removed by Jerry. Richards was able to finish filming the episode.

The character David Lookner was named after "Seinfeld" writer Steve Lookner.

Debra Messing (Beth) is best remembered in "Will & Grace." She was also Miss Junior Rhode Island in 1986.

Cary Elwes (David) breaks character during the dinner scene with Elaine; he mentions his anniversary using his natural British accent.

Elaine's new haircut debuts in this episode. Jerry compares it to the hair of comic strip character Brenda Starr.

134. "The Invitations" (5.16.96)

In the storyline, George is told that a sure way for Susan to call off the wedding is asking her to sign a prenup. This was inspired by Jerry Seinfeld's ex-fiancé Shoshanna Lonstein who called off their engagement after being asked to sign a prenup.

Following the anthrax scare of 2001, syndicated reruns of this episode were suspended over concern that it might seem objectionable and insensitive to use toxic envelopes as the cause of Susan's death. The episode returned to air in the summer of 2002.

New York Yankees owner George M. Steinbrenner III (1930-2010) never actually appeared in a "Seinfeld" episode. He filmed scenes for a guest appearance in this episode but the scenes were deleted. Steinbrenner's scenes involved him taking Elaine out to dinner in anticipation of escorting her to George's wedding. The reason for the deleted scenes remains a mystery: Some report that Steinbrenner objected to Susan's death and asked that his appearance be deleted; the creators' claim the footage was cut due to time constraints; while others claim Steinbrenner was not a good actor and his stiff performance would have detracted from the show. Steinbrenner reportedly missed opening day of the Yankees baseball season to make this appearance.

Larry David knew going into the season that killing off Susan was the only way to properly end the relationship with George. Another possible idea for her demise included having her accidentally impaled by a falling icicle.

The show had mixed reactions; the negative claims related to Susan's tasteless demise (no pun intended) and the characters' apathy. The backlash is mocked in the season premiere "The Foundation" (ep 135) when George and Jerry stand before Susan's grave; Jerry quotes *Star Trek II: The Wrath of Khan* and they become emotional thinking about the death of Spock. Jason Alexander reported that the George character suffered because of this episode and "The Gymnast" (where he eats an eclair that was in the trash). Larry David has since expressed regret is treating Susan's death in a blase manner. Heide Swedberg thought the death and character's reaction was consistent with the show's theme to "express the things the rest of us think but don't want to admit."

Janeane Garofalo (Jerry's girlfriend Jeannie) turned down the role of reporter Gale Weathers in *Scream* (1996) and Monica Geller in "Friends" (both roles then went to Courteney Cox), and the female lead in *Jerry Maguire* (1996) which went to Renee Zellweger.

Barry Marder (Man at Bar) is best known under the pseudonym Ted L. Nancy for writing the "Letter from a Nut" series often linked to Jerry Seinfeld. He also wrote and had a voice role (as Waterbug) in *Bee Movie* (2007) starring Jerry Seinfeld.

Season 8: 1996-1997

Season Regulars
Jerry Seinfeld (Jerry Seinfeld), Julia Louis-Dreyfus (Elaine Benes), Michael Richards (Cosmo Kramer), Jason Alexander (George Costanza)

135. "The Foundation" (9.19.96)

The alley scene featuring the fight between Kramer and his classmates was filmed directly behind the writers' office building.

Jerry Seinfeld assumes the duties as executive producer with the departure of Larry David. This is the first episode to be written and produced without the involvement of David, who departed on good terms, but felt after seven years he was out of ideas for the show.

George yells "Khaaan!" in a spoof of a similar scene involving Captain Kirk in *Star Trek II: The Wrath of Khan* (1982).

One of the things being auctioned off at the foundation is Susan's doll collection, seen in "The Doll" (ep 127).

At Kramer's Karate Dojo there is a picture of martial artist Jackie Chan hanging on the wall.

136. "The Soul Mate" (9.26.96)

This episode features plot elements similar to Edmond Rostand's play *Cyrano de Bergerac.*

In the original script Elaine's boyfriend Kevin was named Fred; however, the change did not occur until after the credits were set.

After Larry David's departure, Jerry assumed more of the responsibility of writing and running the series. Consequently, he ended the traditional opening stand-up routine because it was too time-consuming and he felt his time could be better used elsewhere.

137. "The Bizarro Jerry" (10.3.96)

The concept behind this episode, of having a world made up of everyone's total opposite, is based on the Bizarro World stories featured in Superman comic books. Jerry Seinfeld and episode writer David Mandel are avid fans of Superman.

The "Man Hands" are provided by actor James Rekart. Jerry Seinfeld remembered Rekart from acting classes at the James Best Theatre Center and personally cast him for the role.

The signature "Seinfeld" theme song is played backwards in the tag scene of the episode - another reference to the "Bizarro" theme.

The Bizarro Superman statuette in Kevin's apartment was specially made for the episode. It is now owned by episode writer David Mandel and signed by the entire "Seinfeld" team.

Dana Patrick (Model #1) was the beautiful woman in the Meatloaf video "I Would Do Anything for Love (But I Won't Do That)."

138. "The Little Kicks" (10.10.96)

As the credits role, the final scene uses outtakes between Julia Louis Dreyfus and Jerry Stiller which produced one of the longest laughs ever recorded on "Seinfeld." Filming this scene required many re-takes because Julia Louis-Dreyfus and Jason Alexander were unable to keep a straight face during Jerry Stiller's performance.

Elaine's dance moves were actually her imitating Lorne Michaels from when she was a regular on "Saturday Night Live." The flashback scene of Elaine dancing five years earlier has her character wearing her hair and clothes exactly the way she wore them in season three.

Jerry's line at the end, "I'm still big. It's the bootlegs that got small" is a reference to the movie *Sunset Blvd.* (1950) where Gloria Swanson states, "I am big. It's the pictures that got small."

139. "The Package" (10.17.96)

Wayne Knight parodies his role in *Basic Instinct* (1992) when grilling Jerry about mail fraud.

Phil Hartman makes an uncredited voice appearance as the man on phone who wakes Elaine to confirm the spelling of her surname. Hartman was murdered by his wife Brynn in 1998 in a murder suicide. He is best remembered in "NewRadio," "Saturday Night Live," and 19 voice roles in "The Simpsons." He began as a graphic artist creating artwork for Poco's 1978 "Legend" album, designing the band logo for Crosby, Stills & Nash, and painting the album cover for "America's Greatest Hits: History." Hartman and friend Paul Reubens collaborated to create the Pee-Wee Herman character and Hartman was the voice of Waldo in the Van Halen video "Hot for Teacher" (1984).

140. "The Fatigues" (10.31.96)

Writer's Andy Robin and Gregg Kavet based this story on their experiences as being mentors and protégés at the studio.

It's not a coincidence that the annoying book-on-tape voice sounds just like George Costanza because Jason Alexander recorded the voice-over in an uncredited performance.

The "Seinfeld" logo in the eighth season had a checkered flag background because Jerry intended the eighth season to be the show's last lap. This proved premature; by Christmas 1996 he changed his mind and a ninth season was given the green light.

141. "The Checks" (11.7.96)

When Wilhelm is brainwashed he claims his name is Tania, which is the name Patricia Hearst used after she was allegedly kidnapped and brainwashed by the Symbionese Liberation Army in 1975.

The opening scene of the episode was filmed on September 29, 1996. The scene was also originally intended for the episode "The Fatigues" (ep 140). The second scene was filmed on October 7, 1996, while the third scene was filmed on October 8, 1996.

The last line before the credits had two versions made—one for if the New York Yankees won the World Series and one for if they lost.

Jerry claims to have invented the twirl move done by street umbrella salespeople to attract customers. This is the first non-comedy job Jerry has ever admitted to having on the show.

Gedde Watanabe (Mr. Oh) will forever be remembered as Long Duk Dong in *Sixteen Candles* (1984). In the audition for *Sixteen Candles* Watanabe pretended to only speak Korean and then thanked the casting director in perfect English (he was given the part), and in the movie *Mulan* (1998) another actor did the singing parts because Watanabe's voice was too good.

George Wallace (Doctor) is a comedian and Jerry Seinfeld's best friend, they were roommates in the mid-70s, and he was best man at Jerry Seinfeld's wedding.

Dave Pierce has an uncredited role as Karl Farbman. Pierce worked on "Seinfeld" as the transportation coordinator.

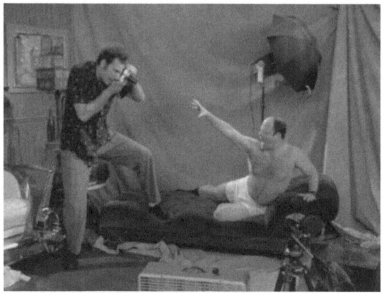

The art of seduction: Kramer (Michael Richards) photographs George (Jason Alexander) in "The Package."

142. "The Chicken Roaster" (11.14.96)

Kenny Rogers Roasters restaurant chain objected to the scene where Jerry accidentally covers everyone's food with rat fur. The writers claimed they would alter the storyline but did not, and Kenny Rogers himself supported the storyline because it was excellent free advertising for his new restaurant chain. He even supplied the cast and crew with a catered dinner.

When Elaine is busted for misusing the corporate account, she says she's "going down like Nixon." She later asks if she can fire the accountant who is pursuing her case. This act parallels Richard M. Nixon's firing of Archibald Cox, the prosecutor who was pursuing Nixon over Watergate.

The scene where Elaine travels to Burma to find J. Peterman is a parody of *Apocalypse Now* (1979) where Martin Sheen meets Marlon Brando for the first time.

Jerry's fear that Kramer's doll, Mr. Marbles, will come to life is a parody of the Chucky doll in the horror movie *Child's Play* (1988).

143. "The Abstinence" (11.21.96)

The working title for this episode was "The Portuguese Waitress."

Wade Boggs was originally included in the script but did not make it into the filming. Instead New York Yankees Derek Jeter and Bernie Williams appear onscreen.

David Letterman's cameo was filmed at his office at the Ed Sullivan Theater in New York.

The effects of Kramer's smoker's lounge led to several minutes of bloopers as Jerry tried unsuccessfully to contain his amusement at Kramer's wretched disfigurement.

Kyle Gass (Smoker) taught Jack Black how to play guitar and they costar as Tenacious D, a two-man rock band. Gass also appears in the Good Charlotte video "Lifestyles of the Rich and Famous."

144. "The Andrea Doria" (12.19.96)

According to writer Spike Feresten, the inspiration for "The Andrea Doria" came from a Central Park tennis club where it was rumored that victims of the Holocaust were doing the scheduling and giving preferential court times to other Holocaust victims instead of regular New Yorkers.

The episode title refers to the SS Andrea Doria passenger liner that collided with the MS Stockholm on July 25, 1956 south of Nantucket Island due to intense fog in the North Atlantic Ocean. Fifty-one people were killed on both ships. The next morning the Andrea Doria sank and slipped beneath the waves. Many ships came to the rescue so that everyone who got off the ship was saved as opposed the disaster of the Titanic that occurred 44 years earlier.

Jerry's line, "Elaine, Newman is my sworn enemy, and he lives down the hall from my home. My home, Elaine! Where I sleep, where I come to play with my toys" is a spoof of Michael Corleone in *The Godfather: Part II* (1974) describing the attack (being shot at) in his bedroom when he says, "In my home! In my bedroom, where my wife sleeps! Where my children come and play with their toys."

Kramer coughing a message to the police is a parody of Lassie saving the day by warning of danger or trouble.

145. "The Little Jerry" (1.9.97)

John Michael Higgins (Elaine's boyfriend Kurt) willingly shaved his head for this role.

The prison yard where George's girlfriend Celia is incarcerated was filmed using the Central Park set at the CBS Studio Center.

A deleted scene shows Jerry and Elaine walking down the streets of New York talking about the difference between a man who's bald and acts bald, and a man with no hair.

Though it's due to a bank error, we learn in this episode that Jerry's checks feature a picture of a clown with balloons. Jerry's full address is also visible on the checks; it reads, "Jerry Seinfeld, 129 W. 81st Street,

New York, NY 10054." On Jerry's bounced check displayed in Marcelino's store, the word "forty" has been misspelled as "fourty."

Jerry's outrage at the price of gum is a parody of the movie *Falling Down* (1993) where Michael Douglas destroys a shop when charged eighty-five cents for a can of soda.

At the beginning of the episode, the camera is pulled back just enough to reveal the actual name of the restaurant (Tom's Restaurant) where the gang always meets. Normally, it is just seen as Restaurant.

146. "The Money" (1.16.97)

Sandy Baron nearly missed appearing in this episode as Jack Klompus because he went into a coma only days before production. Producers searched for a new recurring character but Baron came out of his coma in time to film the episode.

Although Jack Klompus loses the astronaut pen in the swamp, the real Jerry Seinfeld still carries and uses the pen to this day.

147. "The Comeback" (1.30.97)

The tennis court scenes were supposed to use an indoor court but the crew could not find an available indoor court in all of Los Angeles to use as a filming location. Instead they used a massive crane to drape a large tent over an outdoor tennis court to resemble an indoor court. During filming the El Niño weather pattern brought heavy rain to Los Angeles. The rain collected on the tent and several large puddles are visible during the tennis court scene. The tent collapsed shortly after the crew wrapped filming of the master shots; the remaining footage was filmed at the studio on a makeshift half-court set.

In one scene there is dialogue where the main characters are brainstorming the best comeback and George objects that having too many people involved destroys the creative process. This is a direct reference to typical sitcom writing formats where everyone brainstorms ideas in a large group. On "Seinfeld," each writer was responsible for the entire episode and then suggestions were offered late in the process.

In the original script Ben Stein's character was more like Reilly (George's office adversary). The writers decided that Reilly should be a younger, edgier character, so the character was rewritten. Since Stein had been promised a role, the part as a lawyer (Shellbach) was offered to him instead.

The relationship between Elaine and Vincent is a reference to *The Phantom of the Opera* as well as "Beauty and the Beast" where a poetry-reading romantic cat-like beast named Vincent charms a beauty while hidden in the shadows.

In the scene where Jerry locates Milos at the tennis court and observes his horrendous tennis skills, a boom mic is visible at the top of the screen.

148. "The Van Buren Boys" (2.6.97)

The original Kramer story for this episode involved Kramer starting a vending machine business. In the story, he placed the machine outside Jerry's apartment door causing customers to constantly pester Jerry for change and various other things. Kramer selling his stories to J. Peterman was inspired by real celebrities who are notorious for paying for "autobiographical" anecdotes. Kramer sells Peterman his entire library of life stories for $750.

In a final scene which was eventually cut from the broadcast version, Elaine decides to buy stories from Newman but his stories mostly involve eating.

"Seinfeld" writer Steve Koren wanted his name used as a character so it was included in this episode as a boy interested in Susan Ross Foundation scholarship.

149. "The Susie" (2.13.97)

The building in which Susie's memorial took place was actually CBS Studio Center's Building 5, home to the "Seinfeld" writers' and production offices.

Elaine constantly refers to Reggie Miller as "Cheryl Miller's younger brother" which alludes to the siblings' early career. They were both great college and professional basketball players but during his early career Reggie had to deal with being in the shadows of his older sister.

In homage to George's upwards-glancing scream of "Kahn!" in "The Foundation," Elaine screams "Suz!" to the ceiling after hearing that Peterman put her in charge of a foundation in memory of the imaginary Susie.

The lyrics to George's singing phone message are a parody of the theme song to the series "The Greatest American Hero." That song became a top 40 hit for singer Joey Scarbury in 1981.

150. "The Pothole" (2.20.97)

Wayne Knight's line, "Oh, the humanity!" at the end of the episode is a reference to a newsreel quote during the Hindenburg disaster in 1937. Wayne Knight viewed the line as a great mixture of metaphors and it *was* Newman.

The scene where the four main characters are in the janitors closet pays homage to the movie *A Night at the Opera* (1935) where fifteen people crowd into a passenger ship's tiny stateroom.

This is one of Jerry's favorite episodes.

151. "The English Patient" (3.13.97)

The family seen in the movie poster for *Sack Lunch* is actually that of Tim Kaiser, one of Seinfeld's producers. Tim is on the left side with his chin on his hand.

Though his face is never shown onscreen, Neil is played by Jeff Miller, the stand-in for Jason Alexander, who bore more than a passing resemblance to George Costanza.

George's final act of revenge on Neil, disconnecting Neil's IV drip, was ad-libbed by Jason Alexander.

Danielle, the woman who dates a man similar to George, is played by Chelsea Noble who is married to Kirk Cameron. They met on the set of "Growing Pains."

152. "The Nap" (4.10.97)

One of the writers used personal experience to develop this plot because a few of his friends would in fact take naps underneath their desks.

Mitch Mitchell also appears in "The Millennium" (ep 154). The regular George Steinbrenner actor, Lee Bear, was unavailable for these two episodes.

George Steinbrenner's very flawed lyrics to Pat Benatar's "Heartbreaker" song: "She's a heartbreaker, love taker, cruel baker, run this prison like a man. Heartbreaker, love-taker, shoe-maker, won't you cut my shoes for free. Heartbreaker, Brubaker..."

To help George escape an awkward situation, Jerry calls in a bomb threat to Yankee stadium and demands that the next Yankees giveaway be fitted hats, as opposed to the cheaper adjustable hats.

153. "The Yada Yada" (4.24.97)

Peter Mehlman expected "anti-dentite" to be the big catch phrase but "yada-yada" just took off. He came up with the phrase after a woman he knew many years prior used the phrase which he had never before heard. It just sounded funny so he threw it in the script and it managed to get into everybody's speech pattern in the show.

Kramer (Michael Richards) adopts a highway in "The Pothole."

The original uncut version of this episode was well over 26 minutes. NBC allowed the episode to run longer than the usual thirty minutes (with commercials), and its slightly above-average length was even boasted during advertising promos. Nevertheless, cuts had to be made in syndication such as the opening dialog between Jerry and George discussing what to bring on a desert island, additional footage with Kramer and Mickey trying to impress their dates during dinner, and other minor extensions.

The phrase "Yada-Yada" was added to the Oxford English dictionary.

This is one of Jerry Seinfeld's top-five episodes.

Jill St. John and Robert Wagner play the part of Mickey's parents in this episode. In real life, they have been married since 1990.

Jerry Maren (Dad) played the Munchkin who hands Dorothy a lollipop in *The Wizard of Oz* (1939). He played Buster Brown in commercials in the 1950s and 1960s, and Mayor McCheese in McDonald's commercials.

154. "The Millennium" (5.1.97)

The idea for the Putumayo storyline was solidified when a rude florist refused to sell some ribbon to writer Jennifer Crittenden.

It was originally intended to end this episode with a whimsical look at what the year 2000 will be like. The show intended to have Monk's Diner submerged underwater. However, time constraints and cost were the deciding factor.

"Seinfeld" writer Steve Koren plays the role of a young man who is George's top choice to receive the Susan Ross Foundation Scholarship. In an uncredited role, "Seinfeld" writers Spike Feresten, Gregg Kavet, and Andy Robin appear as men outside the stadium.

155. "The Muffin Tops" (5.8.97)

The reality tour storyline was inspired by the real Kenny Kramer who capitalized on the success of his fictional counterpart by offering a "Kenny Kramer Reality Bus Tour" in New York City where he drives tourists to the location of events or places featured in the show while sharing anecdotes about his life.

This episode contains one of Jerry's all-time favorite lines: where he points to his chest and tells George that inside his heart can be found the biggest dating scene in the world.

This is Larry David's final voice role as George Steinbrenner until the series finale because he felt uncomfortable speaking lines written by someone other than him.

George was supposed to work for Tyson Chicken but the company objected to a joke referring to "fermented chicken" and withheld their naming rights. George's employer was changed to Tyler Chicken.

Newman's role as "The Cleaner" is a parody of *Pulp Fiction* (1994) (driving the same black Acura NSX, and giving directions in an imperious way) and *Leon: The Professional* (1994) (bottles of milk rather than acid).

The scene where Jerry leaps off the bus because his chest is itching, then running through the forest and jumping over logs in slow-motion is a parody of the movie *Wolf* (1994) starring Jack Nicholson.

Lippman's reference to "every half-wit and sitcom star has his own book out" is a reference to Jerry Seinfeld's own book *Seinlanguage*.

The title of J. Peterman's autobiography, *No Placket Required* is a parody of the Phil Collins album "No Jacket Required."

156. "The Summer of George" (5.15.97)
The working title for this episode was "The Dude."

A new contract for Season 9 was signed around the time of this airing that would pay Jason Alexander, Julia Louis-Dreyfus and Michael Richards $600,000 each per episode. Until this time they had been receiving $160,000 each per episode. Jerry Seinfeld, as star, co-creator and producer, would continue to receive approximately $1 million per episode.

This episode is, in fact, based on an incident from real life. Faye

Dunaway, who is a contemporary of Raquel Welch, played Norma Desmond in *Sunset Blvd.*, Andrew Lloyd Webber's newest musical at the time. The reviews she received were horrendous and she was consequently fired.

Raquel Welch does a parody of her diva image in this episode. She has a history of being difficult onset. Welch will be forever remembered wearing a cavewoman bikini in *One Million Years B.C.* (1966) that made her a sex symbol. She auditioned for the role of Mary Ann in "Gilligan's Island."

Neil Flynn (Cop #1) is best recognized in "The Middle" and "Scrubs." He auditioned for the role of Dr. Perry Cox on "Scrubs" but it went to John C. McGinley; the role of Janitor was supposed to be for only the pilot episode but his portrayal earned him a permanent cast position.

Six "Seinfeld" team members have uncredited appearances: associate producer Rick Corcoran (Orderly), script supervisor George Doty IV (Man in Restaurant), Judy Kerr (Woman in Restaurant), gaffer Jim Marcos (Man in Café), Pete G. Papanickolas (Man in Café), and Karen Wilkie (Woman in Café). Writer Dave Mandel makes an appearance as the guy who asks George if he wants to play frolf (frisbee-golf).

Season 9: 1997-1998

Season Regulars
Jerry Seinfeld (Jerry Seinfeld), Julia Louis-Dreyfus (Elaine Benes), Michael Richards (Cosmo Kramer), Jason Alexander (George Costanza)

157. "The Butter Shave" (9.25.97)

The storyline involving Jerry and Kenny Bania was inspired by the show's production staff being frustrated over NBC placing inferior sitcoms in the timeslot immediately following "Seinfeld" which turns them into "timeslot hits." Ironically, "Seinfeld" was placed behind the #1 rated show "Cheers" and it became an instant hit thereby preventing its seemingly inevitable cancellation.

The two NBC executives who approach Kenny Bania following his set are named Jay Chermack and Stu Crespi. The names are transposed versions of the NBC executives that developed Jerry's sitcom "Jerry," Stu Chermack and Jay Crespi.

Gordon Jump (Thomassoulo) is best remembered as station manager Arthur Carlson in "WKRP in Cincinnati" and the Lonely Repairman in Maytag advertisements from 1989-2003.

Shannon Whirry (Cute Girl) is best known as starring in many straight-to-video erotic thrillers in the early 1990 (much like genre queen Shannon Tweed).

158. "The Voice" (10.2.97)

The talking stomach was "Seinfeld" writer Spike Feresten's real life experience of imagining his girlfriend's belly button talking to him while she slept. He told the idea to the show's writers who began using the belly button's "voice" as an inside-joke. His girlfriend's reaction was similar to

Claire's reaction in the episode. After being incorporated into the episode, Jerry Seinfeld changed it to Claire's stomach talking to her, so that it wouldn't appear to be simple "body humor." Seinfeld later admitted he wished they had kept it as a talking belly button.

This episode was originally titled "The Backslide."

Kramer's intern Darin was named after former writers' assistant Darin Henry, the unofficial "show mascot" who went on to write several "Seinfeld'" episodes in the final two seasons.

159. "The Serenity Now" (10.9.97)

The plot was inspired by episode writer Steve Koren's real-life experience while driving with his arguing parents. His father shouted "Serenity now!" at the top of his lungs as part of a rage controlling exercise and Koren questioned whether the phrase was meant to be screamed.

The sales contest where the highest seller is rewarded and the lowest is fired is a parody of *Glengarry Glen Ross* (1992).

160. "The Blood" (10.16.97)

Many "Seinfeld" writers thought this episode was so dark that they considered making it a Halloween episode.

The character who dies, Marvin Kessler (whose funeral Jerry's parents come to visit), is a reference to Kramer's original name in the series, "Good News, Bad News" (ep 1).

When Vivian turns on the TV, the screen displays a 'Seinfeld' episode.

161. "The Junk Mail" (10.30.97)

The postmaster general Henry Atkins is played by Wilford Brimley who was a farmer, rodeo rider, blacksmith and bodyguard to Howard Hughes before becoming an actor.

Wilford Brimley, as the Postmaster General, sits on a desk and threatens Kramer. The scenario parodies Brimley's performance in *Absence of*

Malice (1981) where he portrays the Assistant U.S. Attorney General who threatens a room full of lawyers and subordinates using similar statements.

There is a parody of the movie *Three Days of the Condor* (1975) where Newman pulls alongside Kramer and tells him "this is the way it will happen, someone you trust will ask you to get in the car with them," much like Max von Sydow's warning to Robert Redford, and the assassin was dressed as a postman.

The leg uncrossing scene spoofed the movie *Basic Instinct* (1992), where Wayne Knight was the interrogator.

D.A. Johnson (Dirt Person #2) is the uncle of episode director Andy Ackerman.

162. "The Merv Griffin Show" (11.6.97)

Jerry once performed on the real Merv Griffin Show with his fly accidentally unzipped.

When Kramer "takes a break" to warn Jerry about his questionable content, the music he plays is the theme music for the"Jerry" pilot from season four.

Kramer's animal guest is Jim Fowler who was a regular on "Wild Kingdom" (1968-88).

163. "The Slicer" (11.13.97)

At the end of this episode, if you look closely, George still appears in the picture, even though he had already been airbrushed out of it.

George's flashback to the boom box incident occurred in the summer of 1989. This was right after the "The Seinfeld Chronicles" pilot was produced. However, George's 1989 picture has more hair than he had in the 1989 pilot episode.

164. "The Betrayal" (11.20.97)

The idea for a reverse episode was inspired by the Harold Pinter play *Betrayal* which deals with love triangles and has the scenes performed backwards in time. In homage, the creators named Sue Ellen Mischke's fiancé Pinter. The episode has betrayal themes, such as Jerry betrays George by having a relationship with George's girlfriend (Nina), while Elaine betrays rival friend Sue Ellen Mischke by having a prior romance with Pinter.

The subplot involving Kramer originally had him going to India but Peter Mehlman suggested, based on personal experience, that Kramer attends a birthday party in which a person makes a wish. The storyline has Kramer trying to avoid a birthday wish from FDR that he "drop dead." Mehlman and David Mandel agreed to the change in part because of the lollipop gag (where each scene the lollipop gets bigger) and to have Newman involved in the episode.

The entire episode was broadcast in reverse order with the Castle Rock

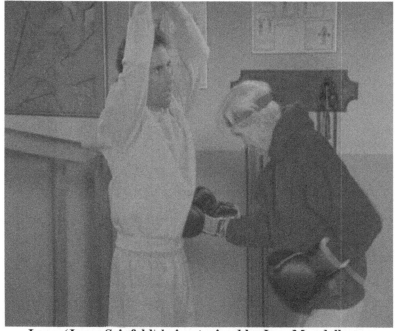

Jerry (Jerry Seinfeld) being trained by Izzy Mandelbaum (Lloyd Bridges) in "The Blood."

logo and end credits running at the beginning, the story being told backwards, and ending with the opening credits. The original airing of this episode was done without the time cards. In syndication they were added to lessen confusion.

This episode's inclusion on the Seinfeld Season 9 DVD is accompanied by a special feature that allows the viewer to watch the episode front-to-back with normal chronology, preceded by a brief introduction from writer David Mandel. This "forward" version has never aired on television.

There were a few deleted scenes: 1) George, staying in India for a few days, is trying to walk off the need to go to the bathroom; 2) Before Elaine hands out the plane tickets, George and Nina are hanging out together; also noting the Timberlands he is wearing at the time; 3) Kramer, coming back to greet Jerry, George and Elaine after the Sue Ellen wedding incident, bumps into a kid who gives him the evil eye before he blows out his candles on his birthday. Because of this, Kramer runs out of the restaurant fearing it will happen again; and 4) On the plane, Elaine tells Nina that she put the fact that Jerry and Nina slept together "in the vault" and then takes the pillow from the man next to her, who turns out to be Vegetable Lasagna (from "The Butter Shave").

Heidi Swedberg (Susan Ross) already had her head shaved for another episode in a different show so she had to wear a wig for this appearance.

165. "The Apology" (12.11.97)

James Spader (Jason) had parents who were teachers yet he dropped out of school and shoveled manure before getting his first acting job.

Jerry's girlfriend Melissa who likes to parade around the house naked is played by Kathleen McClellan who was a former Miss Teen Illinois, 3rd Runner-up in Miss Teen USA 1988 and winner of Miss Photogenic.

Michael Fishman (Gregg) is best known in "Roseanne" as D.J. Conner.

166. "The Strike" (12.18.97)

The idea of a fictitious holiday is based upon Dan O'Keefe's father, who invented his own holiday, Festivus, in 1966 which included all of the traditions except the metal pole (this was added by the writers).

In 2005, based upon this episode, an organization named The Human Fund was established in Cleveland, Ohio.

H&H Bagels was an actual Manhattan company. The "Seinfeld" writers had bagels shipped from Manhattan to their offices every week. The company was forced to close in 2012 when the owner was indicted for stealing $369,000 in employee withholding taxes and evading unemployment insurance taxes.

Soon after this episode aired, Ben and Jerry's Ice Cream released a new flavor called "Festivus," named after the fictional holiday.

This was the final episode to air before Jerry announced the show was ending.

In an uncredited role as Man on the Street, Thomas Azzari worked on "Seinfeld" as the production designer.

167. "The Dealership" (1.8.98)

The scenes where Kramer and the car salesman go on a journey is a parody of the movie *Thelma & Louise* (1991). At the end, they even look a each other, hold hands, and then Kramer steps on the gas pedal.

After his candy line-up is ruined, George screams "Twix" to the sky, in a manner imitative of Captain James Kirk screaming "Khan" in *Star Trek II: The Wrath of Khan*.

The cab driver is played by episode writer Steve Koren.

168. "The Reverse Peephole" (1.15.98)

Jennette Robbins , who plays Jerry's girlfriend Keri, has a line at Joe Mayo's party where she says his pants are "nice." In a Dockers commercial in the 1990s she is on a subway, sees a guy, they get separated, and she mouths the words "nice pants" as the train pulls away.

Joe Mayo is the name of a "Seinfeld" crew member. Knowing this makes it even funnier when Kramer says his name "sounds made up."

During the original broadcast of this episode, one of the commercials featured Jason Alexander advertising the, then new, Intel Pentium II processor.

The inside of Kramer's apartment via the peephole shows a living room immediately in front of the door. However, when Kramer opens the door a wall is in its place, contradicting what the peephole reveals.

169. "The Cartoon" (1.29.98)

The plot involving a cartoon that no one understands was based upon writer Bruce Eric Kaplan's experience having contributed many cartoons to *The New Yorker*. The subplot involving Sally berating Jerry as part of a comedy act is based upon an actual stand-up routine by Kathy Griffin, which was devised after an unpleasant experience as a guest actress on "Seinfeld" (ep 127). During a stand-up performance on "HBO Comedy Half-Hour: Kathy Griffin" (1996), Griffin ridiculed Seinfeld for being rude to her. He was amused and wrote Griffin a humorous letter congratulating her for it and this inspired an idea to write an episode. The two have remained friendly.

The characters repeatedly say the lines, "The New Yorker?" "Yes, the New Yorker." to parody the magazine's advertising slogan at the time.

Newman's comment about Sally's show being about "something" is to counter the fact that "Seinfeld'" has been promoted as "the show about nothing."

George's girlfriend Janet who looks just like Jerry Seinfeld is played by Tracy Nelson who is best remembered in "Father Dowling Mysteries." Her father is pop singer Ricky Nelson ("Garden Party)., her siblings are Matthew and Gunnar from the duo Nelson ("(Can't Live Without Your) Love and Affection"), and her uncle is actor Mark Harmon.

The character Mr. Elinoff is named after "Seinfeld" production assistant Jed Elinoff.

In the episode, Jerry mentioned how he never had a cable special. After "Seinfeld" ended, Jerry was given a cable special, "I'm Telling You for the Last Time" on HBO.

170. "The Strong Box" (2.5.98)

The exterior apartment of Elaine's mysterious boyfriend Glenn is actually located in Manhattan's East Village at 4 St. Mark's Place. Neighborhood landmarks such as Trash and Vaudeville and the St. Mark's Hotel can be seen in the shot.

Jerry's neighbor Phil has the same apartment number (5E) as Newman.

George's girlfriend Maura (she refuses to consent to a breakup) is played by Alex Kapp, who is remembered as Lindsey (one of the mean moms) in "The New Adventures of Old Christine." She first gained notoriety for being the girlfriend of Preppie Killer Robert Chambers, breaking up with him just hours before he murdered his other girlfriend in Central Park in 1986.

The Godfather Part II (1974) is referenced when Jerry accuses Kramer of Fredo's death; to which Kramer exclaims, "Fredo was weak and stupid! He shouldn't have eaten that key!!"

George's request for Maura to "Turn your key!" is a reference to the opening scene of the film *WarGames* (1983) where John Spencer and Michael Madsen are Air Force officers ordered to launch their missiles against Soviet targets.

The woman in the café is Jennifer Eolin who worked on "Seinfeld" as an assistant writer.

171. "The Wizard" (2.26.98)

The "Seinfeld" writers always planned an episode dealing with race, and the initial idea had Elaine getting lost in Harlem but it was abandoned because they simply could not get the tone right.

The Boca Breeze newspaper is filled with front page headlines referring to Larry David; "Larry David gets hole in one!" "Larry David hurts elbow," "Larry David never to play golf again."

A deleted scene features a brief appearance of Bob Saccamano's father who was played by actor Monty Ash.

George says the same line as Michael Keaton, "You wanna get nuts?! C'mon, lets get nuts!" from the movie *Batman* (1989)

Morty Seinfeld protesting that he resigned as condo president instead of being impeached is a reference to Richard M. Nixon, who resigned from Presidency of the United States before he could be impeached.

172. "The Burning" (3.19.98)

The subplot of Elaine discovering David Puddy is religious was based upon writer Jennifer Crittenden finding her husband's car radio tuned to a Christian rock station.

Mickey does a William Shatner impersonation during his "cirrhosis performance."

Julie Wagner has an uncredited appearance as a Medical Student but is better known as the body double for Julia Roberts, Loni Anderson, Nicole Kidman, Lauren Holly and Sharon Stone.

173. "The Bookstore" (4.9.98)

The scene with Newman rolling down the hill in the rickshaw was shot on Bunker Hill in downtown Los Angeles. You can see the One Wilshire building in the background for a few frames, after he collides with Zach. To achieve the wide shot of Newman's rickshaw rolling uncontrollably down the street, the crew hooked the rickshaw to the back of a pickup truck and drove it down the hill, then digitally erased the truck in post-production.

In this episode, J. Peterman referred to opium as "the Chinaman's nightcap." Media watchdog Media Action Network for Asian Americans (MANAA) called on NBC to issue a public apology. NBC did not issue an apology but removed the offending term from the rerun episode.

Jerry Seinfeld's mother Betty appears at Kramer's opening scene party seated next to Kramer as he serves her tea.

The scene where Uncle Leo is shown in jail doing chin-ups is a spoof of

Robert DeNiro's character in the film *Cape Fear* (1991).

Two "Seinfeld" production assistants have an uncredited appearance: Lesley Robins as Zach's Girlfriend, and Frank Sackett as Brentano's Employee.

174. "The Frogger" (4.23.98)

This episode was originally titled "The Cake Parties."

The Frogger machine was actually released in June 1981 so George could not have had the high score in high school (flashback scenes had him and Jerry attending high school in 1973).

While the crew was filming the famous overhead shot of George moving the Frogger game across the street, Jerry Seinfeld noticed that the street was painted with white lines, which was inconsistent with the yellow lines in the Frogger layout. The crew quickly fixed this inaccuracy by covering the white lines with yellow tape.

On September 24, 2005, The Twin Galaxies Intergalactic Scoreboard offered a $1,000 cash prize to the first video game player who could break George Costanza's fictional Frogger high score of 860,630 points. No player was able to break this mark by the December 31, 2005 deadline. However, on December 22, 2009, Pat Laffaye of Connecticut scored a Frogger world record high score of 896,980 points. No other Frogger game has been verified as having beaten George Costanza's score.

The sound effects while George moves the machine across the street are actual sounds from Frogger, played in time with his movements. The sound that plays shortly after the machine is smashed by a truck is the "squash" sound when the frog is hit by a vehicle during the game.

Jason Alexander performed the stunt of diving out of the path of an oncoming truck and being showered with shrapnel from the crushed Frogger machine. He later recounted that two large and heavy pieces of paneling from the side of the game landed uncomfortably close to his head during the shooting of this scene.

On December 27, 2010, a man in Clemson, SC was hospitalized after being hit by an SUV trying to play "real life" Frogger.

"Seinfeld" writer Jennifer Crittenden has an uncredited appearance as Becky. Crittenden briefly dated Jerry Seinfeld in the summer of 1998 between his breakup with Shoshanna Lonstein and meeting current wife Jessica Sklar.

Most of scenes deleted from this episode involve Kramer having a new "long distance" girlfriend, Madeline. This theme carries over to the next episode "The Maid." Christina Haag played the part of Madeline, but is best known as the longtime girlfriend of John F. Kennedy, Jr. in the 1980s.

The brief first exterior shot of Mario's Pizza actually shows a store front with a different name, "Five Roses Pizza." Near the end of the episode a different exterior is shown, and this time the store front is completely different and does display the correct name, "Mario's Pizza."

175. "The Maid" (4.30.98)

In the scene where Jerry offers to rescue Kramer from downtown, Jerry states, "Stay alive. No matter what occurs, I will find you" is a line by Daniel Day Lewis in *The Last of the Mohicans* (1992).

176. "The Puerto Rican Day" (5.7.98)

This is the last episode that involved the writers and all ten contributed to the script; their names are listed in alphabetical order, not based upon contribution. No other series had as many writers for one episode.

Due to controversy surrounding a scene where Kramer accidentally burns and then stomps on the Puerto Rican flag, NBC refused to show it again and it was not initially part of the syndicated package. There were also protests to the portrayal of Puerto Ricans when parade-goers damage Jerry's car and Kramer claims it is like this every day in Puerto Rico. NBC issued an apology.

The traffic jam was filmed at Universal Studios

The character Mrs. Nyhart is named after "Seinfeld" script supervisor

Christine Nyhart. She also appeared in an uncredited role in "The Engagement" (ep 111).

According to Nielsen ratings, this episode was the show's second-highest-rated episode of all time, with 38.8 million viewers, only behind the series finale.

Jerry and the writers had t-shirts commemorating the filming of this episode. On the back was written, "So long, Jackass."

177-178. "Clip Show, Part 1 & 2" aka "The Chronicle" (5.14.98)

This episode was originally titled "The Clip Show" but subsequently renamed for syndication. It is intended to bring the series full circle because the pilot was initially named "The Seinfeld Chronicles."

Both parts of "The Chronicle" were seen by 58.53 million viewers.

This episode aired immediately before the series finale. An outtake of the cast dancing between takes during the filming of the finale is featured here.

To accommodate the long running time of "The Finale," "The Chronicle" ran for 45 minutes on its initial airing. It was expanded to a full hour when rerun.

179-180. "Series Finale, Part 1 & 2" (5.14.98)

This episode originally aired as part of a one-hour-and-fifteen-minute special.

The fake working title for this show was "A Tough Nut to Crack" to throw off outsiders about the contents of the episode. It was more of a challenge to outsiders to figure it out.

Two different verdicts were filmed to keep anyone from being able to give away the real ending to the show.

Jerry once said that the final episode would be about he and George moving LA to work on the show. It seems like they started with that idea in Part 1, and then moved into a completely different direction for Part 2.

The series finale became the first television series to command more than $1 million per thirty second commercial–a mark previously attained only by the Super Bowl.

33 sets were built for this episode, and three sound stages were used.

TVLand paid tribute to "Seinfeld" by not programming any shows opposite "The Finale" so onscreen it had a still shot of a closed office door with the hand written note, "Gone watchin' SEINFELD -- Back in 60 minutes."

Former "Seinfeld" director Tom Cherones can be seen drinking coffee in Monk's Diner during the scene where the gang decides where to fly the NBC jet. Cherones is seated across from then-NBC President Warren Littlefield.

The final episode was watched by 76.3 million viewers making it the third most watched series finale behind "M*A*S*H" and "Cheers."

In 2011, the finale was ranked #7 on the TV Guide Network special, TV's Most Unforgettable Finales.

Jerry's prison cafeteria stand-up act was in fact the last "Seinfeld" scene to be shot. It was thought up during production and filmed two days after the official audience shoot. In the scene, Larry David heckles Jerry, yelling, "You suck. I'm gonna cut you." Meanwhile, Jon Hayman (aka "The Bubble Boy") appears on-camera as the prison guard who escorts Jerry off-stage.

In one scene Uncle Leo is consoling Babs Kramer. However, another scene involving the two of them flirting was cut for time. Interactions between Mickey and Kenny Bania, Newman and Keith Hernandez, and J. Peterman and David Puddy were also filmed, but were cut due to time constraints.

Jason Alexander's real-life wife, Deana E. Title, appears as a juror in this episode.

In the very first episode, the first conversation was between George and Jerry about the location of a button on George's shirt. In the final episode, the last conversation between George and Jerry was discussing the location of a button on George's shirt.

GENERAL INDEX

EPISODE INDEX

Made in the USA
Las Vegas, NV
18 February 2021

18141342R00079